How to Have It All

and

Keep Your Sanity

**ABC's for Success in Business,
Management & Life**

Also by Robin Inwald

ABC's for Inner Strength & Well-Being

Cap It Off with a Smile: A Guide for Making Friends

How to Have It All

and

Keep Your Sanity

ABC's for Success in Business, Management & Life

Robin Inwald, Ph.D.

Hilson Press, a division of Hilson Research, Inc.

New York

Published in the U.S.A. by Hilson Press, a division of Hilson Research, Inc., P.O. Box 150239, Kew Gardens, New York 11415. Phone: 800-926-2258 or 718-805-0063, Web sites: HilsonResearch.com & RobinInwald.com.

Photos by Candace Moore, Design by Robin Inwald & Bill Traynor

Inwald, Robin.
How to Have It All and Keep Your Sanity: ABC's for Success in Business, Management and Life / by Robin Inwald, Ph.D.

Summary: Using the letters of the alphabet, adults are provided with guidelines for success in business, management and life.

Library of Congress Catalog Number: 00-109665

ISBN 1-885738-17-X

1. Self-Help for Business Success – Adult literature 2. Self-Help - Adult

3. Success in Business 4. Business & Management Guidebook

5. How to lead a balanced life

To my daughter, Danielle, who has taught me to meet obstacles directly and with courage.

How to Have It All *and* Keep Your Sanity:

ABC's for Success in Business, Management & Life

A   Ask for What You Need

B   Begin with Behaviorally Based Goals

C   Cultivate Friends

D   Develop Respectful Relationships

E   Exercise, Eat Well and Enjoy the Scenery

F   Favors for Others Will be Returned

G   Go for the Gold

H   Honesty, Integrity, and Accuracy

I   Intense Concentration Brings Results

J   Justify Negative Experiences By Making Them Good

K   Keep A Focus on Discovery & Growth

L   Look to Cut Losses, Then Try, Try Again

M   Motivate Others to Help You

N   Negotiate for 'Win-Win' Solutions

O   One Step at a Time

P   Prepare to Start Over with Permission to Fail

Q   Quit Complaining & Making Excuses

R   Recognize & Reward Colleagues & Co-Workers

S   Stand Out in the Crowd

T   Timing Can Make All the Difference

U   Use Fear to Motivate Action

V   Visualize Yourself as a Winner

W   Words Cannot Harm You

X   X-plore New Ways to Take Responsibility

Y   You Are Where You Are

Z   Zest for Life Gives Us Power

INTRODUCTION

For years I have heard the same question from many different people. "How do you *do* it?" they would ask. During the last few years, my friends have suggested that I write a book about how I have managed to accomplish so much and keep *most* of my sanity at the same time. They think my stories are interesting and tell me that I should share the management tips and insights I have learned. While I am flattered by their suggestions, I know that I have learned just about everything worthy of sharing from those who have gone before me. Maybe I have been a good listener and "borrower" of some good ideas out there. In any case, whatever *else* I know has been learned mainly from the mistakes I have made and not from the successes.

I will relate the stories that periodically resurface in my mind as important lessons and outline the principles I have learned with the hope that you, too, will become a better listener and borrower in your own efforts to develop the skills needed for "getting and keeping it all." It will be satisfying for me, and worth the time spent trying to organize my thoughts, if even a few people use some of these ideas to reach their goals in life. Since this effort is a never-ending process, I hope that I will be able to reread my own book when it is finished in order to remember the things I must continue to do in this universal quest for success. Before I write anything about the ways I have found most useful for "getting *and* keeping it all," I will start by breaking a few "rules."

When psychologists try to assist others in improving their behavior patterns or situation in life, they tend not to reveal who they are while giving this advice. Although they will freely list their credentials and accomplishments for review, they rarely believe it is appropriate to discuss personal successes or failures. This is because therapists and consultants know that should clients learn of the failures they have had in their own lives, they may discount sound advice that is being offered (e.g. "What does that 'shrink' know anyway? Look at the trouble his own son has gotten into!") While this may happen sometimes, I believe that failures teach more than successes and that accepting and analyzing your own failures and those of others is a key to future success. Therefore, I will include personal information and tell you some things about myself before I write about ways I have found most useful for reaching personal and business goals.

Although I know that I have "had it all" for many years now, I also know from personal experience what it is like to "lose it all," too. A little over three years ago, I was on a respirator for three weeks due to life-threatening pneumonia associated with an undiagnosed back tumor that had fractured my vertebrae and would lead to paralysis if not controlled. It *was* as bad as it sounds. When I became conscious again, I discovered that life had gone on without me for almost a month. I could not speak, write, walk, or even lift the phone on the stand next to me. The physical and mental trauma and pain that accompanied me for the next year of treatment and recovery, with the pain ending only six months ago, taught me to better appreciate every day and every detail of my current surroundings.

As for my background, I had the advantage of being born to very bright and hardworking middle class parents who supported me through four years of college. After that, I made my own way. I left my parents' home at the age of seventeen and did not return except for vacations and holidays. This is not to say that I made my way without a lot of help from many people, including my parents. Unfortunately, there is a tendency to think that having had early advantages like this, the rest will follow. As you know from looking around at what happened to the "most popular" or "most likely to succeed" middle class boy and girl from your high school class, this is not always the case. When you consider who would be voted the most "successful" twenty years later, you often find it is a person who was not in the spotlight in high school or even college.

With a great deal of effort over the years, I have achieved successes in several areas through determination, a bit of talent,

2

good luck, and, mostly, hard work and perseverance. In my profession, I have been called a "pioneer" in the field of police psychology for developing the first series of psychological tests validated specifically for screening candidates for high-risk occupations, such as police officers and firefighters. These tests now are used throughout the world for employee selection and fitness-for-duty evaluations. Other tests I developed are used to screen troubled teenagers for violence potential and still others are used for assessing management potential in job candidates for high-level positions in business and industry.

In business, I founded the first female-owned and operated psychological test publishing company in the country and have made sure that this company has stayed profitable for the past twenty-two years. When more than one person bet me that I would not be able to stay in business for one, and then for five years, I managed the challenges, despite having had no formal training in business. I do admit that two years of monthly copies of *Inc. Magazine* served that purpose. I read every word, including the smallest print advertisements. Although I have developed and delivered products for years in this business that are considered "gold class" by male-owned and managed company competitors, my greatest business shortcoming is that I have lacked the know-how or perhaps motivation to "go public" or to build my company to the size of the companies of competitors with less effective and/or respected products.

Aside from building my own company and working with staff to improve our products, services, and sales/marketing efforts, I have spent much of my professional time in the past ten years as an informal human resources consultant to other businesses. Since the majority of our products are used by human resources departments, it was in the natural course of events that I became a provider of information and advice regarding personnel issues. I have had the unique opportunity to sit in what often seems like a central office for human resources directors and administrators throughout the country. The calls for help and discussions about specific employees have given me additional insight about the

3

issues that are of greatest concern in business and management and about the solutions that are most likely to result in success.

On the "let's just call it a hobby for now" side, I am very proud of a few projects I have completed in recent years. After taking several art courses, I wrote, illustrated, and published the children's book, *Cap It Off With a Smile: A Guide for Making Friends*. This book received a series of wonderful reviews, can be purchased at bookstores or through companies like Amazon.com, and regularly sells out in at least one self-help bookstore in Ohio. I also developed an accompanying workbook, school program, buttons, t-shirts, music tapes, and a musical play for children to perform (which they *have* performed in both New York City and Santa Monica, California elementary schools). Despite these efforts, however, I have not managed to find a home and/or wide distribution for the boxes of these books that deserve more than terminal rest in my garage.

When a parent who had read my book suggested that it was the kind of story that would go well with music, I began to indulge in another "let's just call it a hobby for now" project, that of becoming a singer/songwriter and musician. After writing seventeen children's songs to go with the book, and recording them with my three children as the singers, I began to write songs for myself. My past musical experience included studying classical piano and playing flute in the school band.

Since I never had been able to sing well, I decided to take lessons to see if it was possible to sing without scaring the neighbors. Now I have completed my second full-length CD of original music. I am proud to say that I sang every note on both CDs without mechanical pitch correction, which is currently a common practice. Now I regularly perform my songs with other musicians in public places and even have a web site under my name so that people can listen to my recordings. The "down-side" of this effort is that there is not enough time to practice, write, record, and find ways to distribute my music along with everything else. Learning patience and enjoying the moment,

4

regardless of the result, are areas where I need continued practice.

Despite the achievements listed above, raising children has been the most challenging *and* the most rewarding experience in my life. Since my children have grown up at the same time as I have been "raising" my business, I have had the opportunity to discover the many parallels between helping a child to grow into an adult and managing employees as they grow in their careers.

My initial training as an educational/school psychologist did not adequately prepare me for the real life experience of handling a child who has "forgotten" to do a major school project or who comes home to relate calmly that some friends have been out buying drugs. My nine-year long part-time job as a clinical psychologist in a hospital's phobia clinic for adult patients did not adequately prepare me for handling an employee who did his job, yet enraged the rest of the staff. Nor did it prepare me for the disgruntled police officer who impersonated a police chief on the Internet and complained about my company's "bad tests" to our real police chief clients. In fact, we had properly helped his agency to promote a more qualified applicant for the position of sergeant and this officer's behavior only verified his own poor test results. Of course, *nothing* can adequately prepare parents for what is in store with teenagers in the house anymore than managers can be prepared to deal with an angry ex-employee wielding a gun.

Especially since parenting is an ongoing process, it is not unlike managing employees in business over the long-term. Many parents who are in their seventies and eighties continue to provide advice and guidance to their "children" no matter what their age is at the time. The one thing you can count on is that children are constantly changing. Just when a parent has one stage somewhat under control, another one pops up. Likewise, the needs of employees change over time as does the business climate. Therefore, the knowledge and management skills needed by human resources managers and other administrators must expand to meet new legal and cultural staff requirements in any company.

In parenting as in business management, I have learned that the old saying, "Garbage in, garbage out," is particularly accurate. In general, if management problems are ignored, they only will multiply. Conversely, when an investment is made in other people, all concerned will enjoy positive benefits, whether in business or in family life. Since good management or good parenting techniques that result in the successes of others also bring success to the manager or parent, I will include information regarding parenting strategies with the hope that managers in business who also are parents can improve upon strategies and techniques that are helpful in both areas.

The parental experiences I have shared with my husband have been enhanced recently as all three of our teenagers have achieved major accomplishments in their academic, musical, and athletic activities. I think it is important to realize that although *potential* for special abilities and talents may be inherited, my children were no different from others in their natural inclinations. Left to their own devices, I believe that they would have been content to watch TV, play computer games, and e-mail their friends throughout their early school years. Their rooms stay messy. You can't walk *in* to one of them. They don't leave the bathroom ready for even *their* guests. Their choice of clothing and hair color is idiosyncratic, to say the *least*. All three have a group of friends to "hang out with" and love eating junk food. However, homework and music were the activities that I chose to make mandatory. In addition, the guidance to find their different talents and passions *and* to develop them was most deliberate.

Although I could not foretell the specific areas where my children would be able to do well, I did pay careful attention to the ways in which they approached their activities and interests. While talent or potential may be inborn, and parents do control the opportunities, or lack thereof, for their children's growth, rewarding both practice skills and signs of a child's self-motivation is key to the development of long-term focus in areas where good things can be achieved.

I have helped, and continue to coach, my children on how to manage their time efficiently so that they will have free time and can avoid "burn out." Throughout all of their activities, it is important to note that there has been time left for birthday parties, hanging out at the mall, and visits with grandparents and family as well. Also, participation in extra-curricular activities always has been contingent upon grades that reflected the children's best efforts in school.

Motivating other people to achieve goals at work, the main job of a good manager or business owner, and placing employees in positions where they can perform well so that a business will prosper, are not unlike the careful guidance a parent can give to a child. Regardless of status, whether student or employee, the recipe is the same. With hundreds, maybe thousands, of books on management and lifestyle available, I only attempt this one with the hope that my unique experiences can add validation to those management principles that work.

As part of my job, I have conducted and published research on personality characteristics that are associated with success in many different occupations, from security officer to police chief, from office assistant to sales manager to company president. Thanks to this research, I now have a good idea of why I, and others close to me, have missed some important opportunities due to deficits in one or more of these important traits. I do believe, however, that most people have the potential to get what they really want if they focus on their best qualities and make time for the concentrated practice of skills I will outline in this book. Unlocking potential is the hard part, not finding that it exists!

In this book, I have listed ABC's for success in business, management and life that I practice and preach to myself. While there are exceptions to every rule or idea of how to do something in the most efficient or effective way, these ABC's provide a method for maximizing potential *and* saving yourself from "burn-out" at the same time.

A – ASK FOR WHAT YOU NEED

"Ask for a Present in Both Your Life and Dreams"

It is never easy to ask others to give you things. Most parents try to raise their children to be largely self-sufficient, which is, by definition, the state of not needing to depend on others in order to survive. Some people have the impression that asking for something lowers their status by putting them in an inferior position. "Rich and powerful people don't have to ask for anything"…or do they actually ask for things the most? It certainly is the salesperson's most important task to "ask for the sale" and those who cannot manage to do this on a daily, and sometimes hourly, basis are bound to fail in this role. Owners and managers in businesses must ask for things as well. Holding back when they need something from others, such as bank loans, contacts, or important information, can have a serious negative impact on a company's bottom line.

An interesting story has been told about an Indian tribe known for the good mental health of its members. When children in this tribe had nightmares, their parents told them to turn to the monster or bad guy and "ask for a present or gift." This shift in a bad dream may have the effect of refocusing the plot and putting control back on the dreamer's side.

Likewise, being able to ask for what you need or want in your business and personal life is very important. If you do not express yourself clearly, or are too shy or afraid to let your wishes be known, those who can help you will not know exactly what to do. Worse, someone else may ask for what you want and get it only because you failed to let it be known that you wanted it too. "Monsters" can be eliminated, or at least their impact reduced, when you *take control* over your own life and dreams. Even if what you ask for is refused, putting your interests on the table may help you to revise your strategies and achieve your goals at a later time.

The idea that you rarely lose anything by asking, and should go ahead and ask most of the time regardless of outcome, was a business lesson I learned fifteen years ago when I was trying to obtain a testing contract with a large security company. At that time, most of my company's contracts were with public law enforcement agencies. We had a few small security companies who were using our tests. At a trade show, I met a branch manager who had previously used and liked our tests when he was with a smaller company. Now he was working for one of the larger companies that did not have any testing program in place. He invited one of my staff members and me to a party given by his new company and offered to introduce me to his company president. Later that night, I sought him out at the party and he did introduce me to his president.

I took the company president's business card and, unlike my usual pattern of following up weeks later due to other more pressing business matters, I typed a letter to the man the president had told me I should contact as soon as I returned to my office. I knew that they did not have a testing program and that if I were the first person to reach the right people in that company, I would have a chance of working with them if they ever *did* start a program. In the letter enclosed with my company's literature, I simply asked if a psychological testing program were ever to be considered, that my company be given an opportunity to present our materials and submit a bid.

A year passed and I never heard back from this man. I did not want to "bother" him or the president since I thought that my letter was enough. I also thought that I might seem too eager and even annoying if I tried to make additional contacts. After all, since I didn't think the company had hired anyone else to do the work I was proposing, I figured that it would be best to remain "low-key." Of course, I now believe that I was wrong and that this is a very inefficient method for increasing business. In any case, I was afraid to ask for the sale and afraid to bother the man with questions about whether he even had *thought* about developing a testing program in his company.

The next year, at the same annual convention, I bumped into the branch manager who had made the first introductions. He informed me that his company had just made a deal with one of my competitors to develop a testing program. I was floored. As it was, I rarely had the time to type individual proposals to anyone and I had made what I considered to be a special effort in order for my company to have a bidding opportunity.

After deciding that it was better late than never, I immediately left my booth at the convention and went searching for this company's president. I found out when he would be at his company's exhibit and made sure that I was there at that time. When I saw him, I launched an all-out "attack." Very nicely, I reintroduced myself and reminded him of how we had met and of the letter I had written to his staff member, just as he had suggested. It turned out that his staff member had died during the year and someone else had taken his position.

I then told him how I had heard that they had contracted with a competitor and listed all the reasons why they should, *at least*, have given us a chance to bid. I was so clearly enthusiastic about my tests and so concerned that I hadn't had an opportunity to bid, that this company president was impressed. He said that he would "look into it" and get back to me the next day. I had done my best under the circumstances, but figured that nothing would happen after that.

The next day, this man found my company's booth and told me that his company had *not* made any final decisions yet, since he had not been informed about the arrangement with the other company before we had spoken. It did not hurt that when he visited the competitor's booth after talking to me, without revealing which company he represented, the staff member at that exhibit appeared disinterested in talking about her products and then rudely blew cigarette smoke in his face.

I did have the opportunity to present our testing materials and we eventually gained a new customer that became one of our larger accounts. For many years, I consulted with this company and my company prospered due to the effort. I learned my lesson about asking for what I needed in a direct and timely manner. Of course, I was lucky that I had a second chance to do my asking. In business dealings, especially, this often is *not* the case.

I have seen many situations where people are hesitant to ask for what they need and are passed over in favor of someone else because of it. Part of this may be due to the old saying, "It's the squeaky wheel that gets the grease." I saw one example with a manager who had worked for a large company in Washington for over ten years. He was in a middle management position and was able to support his family on his salary. However, he watched as other managers left the company for better paying jobs and saw some of his colleagues get promotions or larger salary raises than his bosses were giving him.

After a long wait, perhaps to see if his bosses would "come around on their own," he finally placed his resume with a headhunter. It was only when he was offered a position with another firm that his company came up with a counteroffer of more pay and increased benefits. While he considered staying with his old company, the headhunter pointed out that if they hadn't given him the raise and advancement until they thought they would lose him, they probably wouldn't treat him very well after awhile if he stayed. He left the company with the feeling that he "should have asked" for the raise years ago.

Of course, asking for what you need requires certain skills, too. A competing test company's sales manager used one of my psychological tests because he was having trouble with his sales staff. He wanted to know what my tests could offer that the sales testing products from his own company could not. One saleswoman, in particular, was not performing well. She was calling and talking to customers, but could not "ask for the sale" and rarely brought in new customers. However, she appeared to be a very pleasant, extroverted, and people-oriented person to her boss. He thought that would be enough to make a good salesperson.

The test results showed that she had a history of having a very difficult time learning new information in school and at work and that she had unusually low self-confidence, far below the average for other sales personnel we had tested previously. This woman was selling an academic product to professionals who were constantly asking her to explain the validation research connected with these tests. The combination of not being quick to learn new information and having poor self-esteem created a situation where she was likely to be intimidated by her customers. When the sales manager interviewed her more carefully, he discovered that the testing had been accurate. She admitted that she would back out of a sales conversation whenever it became "too academic" and usually didn't "ask for the sale" either, thinking, "Who would buy a product from *me,* anyway?"

My suggestion would have been to develop a more comprehensive training program for this company's products with more literature than they used to distribute so that salespeople would not have to remember so much technical information. I also would have recommended that the company send this particular saleswoman to an assertiveness training program. However, since the sales manager was satisfied with the testing and didn't *ask* my opinion, I didn't volunteer it. After all, he was a competitor!

Finally, it is very important that when you do ask for something, you consider the person you are asking. What is it that granting your request can do for that other person? If you are asking for a raise, how will your work warrant that raise? What new project can you spend extra time and effort completing? What do you bring along with your request that will help the person you hope will help you? Here's an example of a situation when I asked for the wrong thing and it backfired.

Early in my career, when I had been working in my business for only two or three years, I brought what I thought was some very interesting research to the commissioner of a large correctional agency. I had discovered, through analyzing both pre-employment psychological test data and resignation/termination rates of hired correctional officers, that the officers with the most emotional adjustment difficulties tended to stay the longest on the job and rarely resigned. This was the group with the largest percentage of termination for cause as well. These results could be interpreted to mean that the people with the most problems, but who didn't get into enough trouble to be fired, would try to hold onto their jobs the longest, perhaps out of fear that they could not find or hold a job somewhere else.

I also discovered that the officers with the least problems, as evidenced on their psychological exams, showed the greatest percentage of resignation. I thought that this research would convince department administrators that they should try to find out why their best people were leaving. I thought wrong. I then made the mistake of asking the commissioner to authorize the development of programs to encourage special assignments and earlier promotions for the good staff members who were leaving. I was nearly laughed out of the office.

In fact, I actually was asking this commissioner to do something that his bosses had no intention of letting him do. The pressures on this administrator were coming from a large city government that wanted to reduce overtime and reduce the hiring of new employees at all costs. Long-range planning was not in the picture here, as I soon learned is the case in many government-run organizations. Instead, the needs of politicians who appoint commissioners, and promise to meet certain budgetary goals, must be met before any innovative programs can be introduced.

In this case, my good intentions were misunderstood. The commissioner was happy with the results of my research. He told his staff that, from then on, they should *not* hire the better-suited people since "they would leave anyway" and should concentrate, instead, on hiring the people who were most likely to stay on the job (i.e. the ones with the most psychological disturbances!)

Even if a certain percentage of these more troubled officers later were fired, this commissioner thought that this was a good way to reduce overtime and turnover, due to the high percentage of resignations on the part of the more stable officers. If this logic sounds strange to you, it is interesting to note that this same issue came up in a police department several years later. The police chief there openly admitted that he had ordered the rejection of police officer candidates who scored too *high* on an IQ-type test since they were not likely to *fit in* with the other officers and, therefore, were more likely to leave the department sooner than other officers.

Clearly, I had stepped, unknowingly, into a situation with this commissioner that I could have avoided. I did not want my research to result in a public safety agency hiring the least qualified officers to avoid the resignations of those who were more qualified. However, I had not considered the needs of this director or how doing the *opposite* of my request actually would help meet *his* needs in the department. A more careful and creative approach may have worked if I had presented a clear explanation of exactly how my ideas would result in less overtime and turnover in the future and the hiring of fewer new people in the department.

Another time, my willingness to ask for something I actually did not think I could get really paid off. I was searching for an apartment in New York City and was looking for a job at the same time. I had a job interview in an office in a centrally located building near Lincoln Center that had both residential and commercial apartments. After the interview, I was so impressed by the office that I asked the building's manager to show me any apartments that were available. The empty apartments were either too small or too expensive, but the manager showed me a beautiful rooftop terrace shared by the building's tenants. That evening, I went to the movies with a friend in the same neighborhood. I decided to show my friend the building and we walked into the lobby without being stopped by the doormen. Since we were already inside, I thought it would be fun to go up the elevator to the roof terrace.

In the elevator, I asked a tired-looking businessman who was coming home from work which floor had the roof terrace. He said, "That's on my floor. I'll show you the way." As we rode to the twenty-first floor, I asked this man how he liked living in the building. When we arrived on his floor, and he put his key into the door of the apartment in front of the elevator, I asked if he would mind if we just peeked inside for a moment so that I could show my friend how nice the apartments were in the building. Surprisingly, he said, "Fine," and we went inside. We were just in time to see a beautiful orange and pink sunset over a cityscape of buildings from the window of his large living room. There was classical music playing and this man's wife was waiting with two glasses of wine on a tray. Their cat was lying on the carpet, basking in the glow of the sunset. I gushed over how gorgeous I thought their apartment was and they offered us wine in return.

As we got up to leave after a brief visit, I jokingly asked, "How would you like to move out and give me your apartment?" With complete seriousness, the man said that he and his wife actually were planning to move to Connecticut but had a lease on their current apartment until the end of the year and didn't think they could break it. I couldn't believe my ears. This couple was paying less rent for their large apartment than the rents for the much smaller apartments I had seen earlier that day in the same building. I suggested that we both go to the manager and tell him that I would take over the apartment and that he could raise the rent to the next legal level right away. When the manager later said that he couldn't do that, and that I would have to go on the waiting list like everyone else, the tenant told him that they wouldn't move out early unless I was the one who got the lease to their apartment. Motivated by the opportunity to collect the increased rent money for a few months, the manager finally relented and gave me the apartment.

Several years later, the apartment building became a condominium and tenants were able to buy their apartments at the low "insider" prices. Over twenty years later, my husband and I still own this beautiful apartment. We have rented it at a profit and have saved it for ourselves or for our children to use in the future only because I had the nerve to ask for something in the most unlikely of circumstances.

On a final note, make sure that you do your asking in front of the right people. Sometimes it is very difficult to know *whom* to ask since organizations often protect their decision makers. This may require some preliminary research on your part, but it is well worth the effort. I cannot count the times earlier in my career when I spent valuable time trying to convince someone to make a decision about buying my company's services or products, only to find out that he or she was not in the department where this type of decision could be made!

In addition, it is not an infrequent occurrence for certain staff members in an organization to believe that they have the power to make decisions when they do not. The best strategy is to ask directly if the person you are speaking with has the authority to make the decision regarding your type of request. If not, ask to be introduced or directed to the person who does. Finding out more information about a company's internal structure in advance also can help you to find the right person to ask.

To implement the **"A" for "Ask for What You Need"**:

1. Make a resolution always to ask for what you need. You rarely will lose anything important merely by asking for something.

2. Remind yourself to ask only the person who has the power to assist you.

3. Ask for what you need with the offer of giving something back that is useful to the person you are asking.

4. Write down ten things you would like to have that someone else has the power to give you. Before this next week is over, ask directly for at least two of them. Include what you will do in return that will increase your chances of receiving a "yes" answer.

B – BEGIN WITH BEHAVIORALLY BASED GOALS

" A Boat That Has No Port-of-Call Will Never Find Its Home"

What students learn in business schools and what entrepreneurs learn when they start their businesses often seem worlds apart. While it always is important to know where you are headed, the actual course rarely can be correctly charted ahead of time. Many successful businesses might not have been started in the first place if full-blown "business-school" techniques and analyses had been carefully applied. This is because some business ideas that are far-fetched and "high risk" eventually produce the greatest returns and it is difficult to predict which of these will be most successful.

Some businesses do not begin with a set of clearly stated goals. This was the case in my own company. Without any thought in my head that I would ever start a business, I had developed a psychological test and conducted research that showed how well it worked compared to other tests available at that time. I had started this project as a way to help myself do a better job in screening candidates as a consultant to a local law enforcement agency. I brought my test to a psychologist working for a large and well-established test company who thought it would be a very good addition to his company's catalog. I thought that I would let his company market my test since it already was marketing a test written by one of my graduate school professors. I expected to earn an eight or ten percent royalty on tests sold and to move on to the next events in my life.

To my disappointment, when this psychologist presented my test to the corporate decision-makers in his company, they rejected it. The comments in their "no thank you and don't try again" letter included their view that "there was no market in the public safety/law enforcement field for this kind of testing" and "people would not answer these types of questions honestly even if there were such a market." I already knew that this board of test "experts" was wrong on both counts. I had conducted research studies that verified the test's predictive validity and knew that I had developed the questions directly from questions the candidates already had answered willingly both in individual interviews with me and on written pilot tests. Because of this rejection, I was determined to find another way to publish my test and to make it available to other psychologists and test users. I was motivated by a desire to prove that what I had developed *did* have a market and *would* work, not by a specific desire to start a business.

Next, I approached a psychologist and owner of a new test publishing company. He met with me and liked the project, accepting my test for his catalog. When he informed me that I would have to supply him with the completed manuscript for the test's technical manual in addition to the brief summary and pile of research data I had presented to him, I realized that it was going to be up to me to do most of the preparatory work, no matter which company published it. I had been looking for outside publishers with the misconception that *they* would pull the information together for me. I also realized that, if I had to do it myself anyway, maybe I could call a company to print the manual and market the test myself with ads in the American Psychological Association's monthly newspaper. This would give me one hundred percent of the royalties, rather than ten percent, once I covered expenses. I planned to pay for the ads from profits earned in the direct services contracts I held with a few local public safety agencies. Luckily, I had no idea that the most expensive and difficult task in business is not *making* products, but marketing and selling them!

Perhaps because of my ignorance, I proceeded to develop my first test manual and a business of my own. The idea of incorporating as a legitimate company actually came from my contract supervisor in the law enforcement agency where I was working. She made the suggestion that I start a business where I could hire consultants. This agency needed additional staff, but was not willing to go through the tedious paperwork and difficulty it would have as a government agency in laying off employees when there was less work required in the pre-employment testing unit. Therefore, my supervisor thought it would be a good idea for me to hire consultants who could be employed through my contract whenever work was available.

As a result, I started my company for an unusual reason, to help a city agency avoid hiring additional employees. When I had developed the manual for my test nine months later, I already had a company in place through which to market my new product. Everything seemed to be fitting into place and I didn't know enough to write down specific goals for my company at that time. I did not write a formal business plan, though I did make periodic lists of what I wanted to do next, such as "hire a new employee" or "write a new test." I was proud of the fact that I was not a business school graduate, yet had a company that became profitable within three years. What I didn't realize was that my "boat was floating in the ocean without a plan of where to dock."

Whether business plans are formalized or not, there are very specific goals in the minds, if not on paper, of every successful entrepreneur/manager who sets up shop. The often-stated ultimate goal of business owners and their managers is to "make money." For some people, that seems to mean the opposite of reaching for goals geared to "helping people" or "providing something useful to society." Once, a staff writer for *Inc. Magazine* suggested to me that "professionals," such as physicians, dentists, architects, and engineers, make terrible business owners and managers precisely because they become caught up in professional issues and fail to make logical business plans for their companies.

Some business owners and managers never really assess their goals and where they want to end up in their careers. While it is possible to conduct a business without a major plan, this course often leads to confusion and limited growth. This is what happened in my case. Luckily, I was in a niche market where I could provide a somewhat unique service. In highly competitive fields, this course can spell disaster.

About ten years after I started my business, a competing test company's owner and president expressed his view that I had let professional concerns hurt my own and other test company's revenues. I had published an article about how validation studies should be done and had exposed the weaknesses of companies that did not conduct what I considered to be adequate research before selling tests. In our conversation, I realized that his business goal had been "to make money" whereas I had earned income by default, as a result of "trying to be a good professional developing useful services for colleagues and earning a living at the same time." When I told him we had started with different goals, he laughed at me in disbelief and said something to the effect that I was a "very good actress."

When this man met his stated goals a few years later and sold his company for millions of dollars, I realized that our different "business" versus "professional" goals had a major effect on outcome, regardless of the fact that I had not written mine on paper. He had made a fortune by selling tests with less research and more marketing, whereas I had a much smaller, though highly respected, business with what I believed to be "better" products that were not nearly as profitable. At that time, I realized that if I had consulted with experienced business owners and developed a more comprehensive plan, I might have been able to combine my professional goals with some specific business-related goals that would have helped my company to grow without sacrificing the integrity of its products. Without such a plan, I had "floated around in my boat," never reaching any particular business port-of-call.

More recently, I have had the opportunity to consult with a friend of mine who has been building a quilting business out of her home for the last six years. What first began as a hobby has now developed a life of its own and she describes herself as "strung out" trying to fill the unexpected volume of new orders as they are received. The growing pains of this new business now have reached the critical point where it is time for her to make some important decisions. These decisions will depend on what she decides are her ultimate goals for herself and her business and how much time she wishes to devote to her work in the future.

When speaking about this business, my entrepreneurial friend said that people were telling her to make a business plan. While this may not be her first priority at the moment, the need to set specific goals and to think ahead to what she envisions five or ten years from now is essential for her future happiness and continued satisfaction with her business. Regardless of the accuracy of her projections, she will have a plan to follow and a vision of where she wants to go even if it is for the short-term.

If my friend wants to expand to be able to fill more orders for her customers, she will have to delegate much of the actual quilting work to others. This will mean giving up the fun of creating each quilt herself, but then she will have the time to work on expansion activities. Having experienced frustration at *not* examining these issues more carefully in my own business, I have suggested that she take the time now to decide how she wants her business to look in the future and how much of her personal or borrowed resources she is willing to devote to this venture.

Just as a reformed smoker or alcoholic preaches abstinence to all who will listen, I also admit to my past "goal-less" tendencies and try to help others avoid my previously winding and wayward path. A few years ago, my company developed an instrument to help human resources departments identify their goals in selecting new employees. Using a simple questionnaire, administrators, as well as job incumbents, could rate various characteristics as "essential," "important" or "not important" for employees in specific positions in their companies.

It was interesting to find that, although administrators within many organizations *thought* they had common goals in the type of personnel they wanted to hire, they often did not agree on the basic characteristics that are most important to identify in the screening of their job applicants. Using this questionnaire as a starting point for discussing the most important areas to assess in the selection process has had an immediate and significant positive effect. Of course, it is important to realize that if you try to screen for more than a few characteristics, you may not find *anyone* to hire. However, once administrators agree on the most important areas of focus, hiring goals are reached more quickly with less confusion and internal misunderstandings.

Another example of the need to fully develop a vision of the end result occurred when one organization hired human resources consultants and psychologists to solve a problem without anticipating the situation that would arise from its solution. In this case, a judge had ordered a correctional agency to develop a testing process that would screen out all applicants who showed "sadism, brutality, or racism." The organization hired external "experts" at great expense and told them to develop such a test. Without first examining the characteristics that were necessary for good officers to have in order to successfully do their jobs, the true "goal" of this project, these consultants developed a test that screened out individuals who showed assertiveness, "authoritarianism," and a few other supposedly-related personality characteristics.

When I questioned the commissioner in this agency a few years after this customized, yet unvalidated, test had been introduced, he lamented that now his agency was having serious problems because the new officers *lacked* necessary assertiveness. Life-threatening incidents were occurring with alarming frequency and his command staff had observed that many new employees were "scared to death of the inmates." While it may have seemed like a noble effort to screen out "sadism, brutality, and racism," consultants had missed the mark by not finding out which characteristics were necessary in order for officers to do their jobs and maintain necessary "care, custody, and control" of the inmates.

Actually, there is no validated way to screen for such characteristics anyway. Public safety administrators cannot and will not clearly identify enough "known" sadists or racists within their departments so that their profiles can be compared with those of "non- sadists." The result of this misguided effort was that it eventually was abandoned. In the end, setting clear and reachable goals, while carefully examining possible alternatives, is the most efficient way to avoid disappointment and to reduce the chances of eventual failure.

I recently heard the story of one large manufacturing company that jeopardized its prominent position in the marketplace after it developed a new product that was not within its usual line. Since there were no clear goals set in this company, enterprising employees who had developed this new product forged ahead on their own and cultivated new business. Just when the product began to bring in new customers and revenues, the company's executives decided to cut back on overhead costs. Without checking with their staff, the first thing they cut was the new product, saying that it wasn't in their traditional line of business. This made the new customers angry, since they had been consulting actively with the company's employees on how to develop a useful set of products they later could purchase. When the company suddenly reversed this momentum by saying that it no longer was in that business, ill will was created among the new clients.

A few months later, these same executives changed their minds when they realized that other similar companies had begun to offer the new product line. By this time, however, the damage had been done. Now it was necessary to restart the manufacturing process from the beginning, only to find that the new customers already had switched their allegiance to different product providers. All of this could have been avoided had the company's executives polled its employees, conducted thorough market research, and developed clear long and short-term goals for the business.

To implement the **"B"** for **"Begin with Specific Goals"**:

1. List three specific goals you would like to reach within the next year. Then list three specific goals you would like to reach within the next five years.

2. List the steps you will have to take in order to reach each of these goals. Be as detailed as possible.

3. Give each step a reasonable deadline that you can meet.

4. List and evaluate the importance of the things you may have to give up in order to reach each of these goals, such as losing time with family in order to complete a degree in school.

5. Rank order the goals in order of their importance to you for one and then five years. Begin to complete the first step in next year's first ranked goal today.

6. Dedicate a notebook for writing your goals and the steps you will take to reach them. Give yourself a place to check off when you have completed each step and try to review your notes at least once every month.

C – CULTIVATE FRIENDS

"It's Not Only What You Know But Who You Know"

Once a company's products or services are established, the relationship between the service or product provider and the end user is the critical link that allows a business to expand and to enjoy years of success. This relationship is not very different from the one that develops between friends in a social setting. In fact, good friends receive things from each other that enrich their lives and good business relationships are much the same.

I once met a man on an airplane who I would describe as a super salesman. He and his girlfriend, also a salesperson, were sitting next to me and we talked for four hours on our grounded plane before it managed to let us off at the same airport where we originally had boarded. When we were told that we had to stay overnight in very poor accommodations (this was the only hotel I ever stayed in where my feet actually stuck to the carpet), a group of passengers decided to make a bad situation into a party. We shared food and stories all evening and, by the next day, we felt like old friends who had gone to camp together.

What was most interesting about this experience was that, through the frank talk that sometimes comes when strangers meet on buses or planes for a short while, I learned how at least one salesman managed to make over half a million dollars in commissions each year. It is an approach to work that is not difficult to understand, but requires some discipline and a great deal of time to implement. It involves the making of friends.

This super salesman sold boxes, mostly labeled packaging for products that would be mailed to customers. Such items are certainly commodities that can be provided by many companies and are not difficult to design. However, this salesman was able to earn his unusually high income by purposely cultivating friendships as a full-time career. He explained to me how he saw his clients as friends, viewed every potential customer as a possible friend-to-be, and that his main goal was to improve on his relationships with his clients every chance he got.

For now, he and his girlfriend were not planning to have children since they were devoting nearly all of their time to entertaining, meeting with clients, and telemarketing. He described how he would find out which hobbies a potential client liked and then try to find a way to participate in that hobby with the person. If he could obtain a sporting event ticket for the client, this was just the beginning. Business dinners, weekend picnics, and eventual attendance at family events of some of their clients were typical activities for this couple. They admitted that their business lives were merged almost entirely with their personal lives but said that, since they were having such a good time, they didn't mind this situation. What impressed me the most was that both members of this couple were low-keyed, almost subdued and modest in their personality styles, though high-keyed, genuinely interested, and fully focused regarding their ability and desire to create long-lasting friendships with clients. They clearly loved their work, their friends who were also their business associates, and each other.

Meeting this couple reminded me of my summer job after high school graduation. I sold cookware door-to-door and found my potential clients through engagement announcements in the local newspaper. One time, I had a problem with a customer who bought a set of my cast iron pots but was denied credit after I made the sale. Although this family had told me over the phone that they were going to cancel the order, my supervisor told me that I should ask if we could stop by their house once more. After dinner the next evening, my supervisor came inside with me to talk with the family whose daughter had wanted the cookware set for her upcoming marriage.

I then watched this man, a master salesman, change the whole scene by talking with the family for awhile. After asking a few questions, my supervisor was able to find a common area of interest and experience with the young woman's father. Soon he and the father were engaged in a very serious conversation about their different experiences in the service during the Korean War. Before long, the father went to a drawer and pulled out some cash to pay directly for his daughter's cookware. She was very happy and I saw the power of social interactions and their direct relationship to business deals. Making friends, or at least making a social connection in business, really is the key to successful negotiations and conflict resolutions.

For example, one of my friends wanted to sell her mother's condominium in Florida and a real estate broker quickly found her a potential buyer. Even though this buyer originally said that he wanted to purchase the apartment, he did not sign the contract for several weeks. When my friend realized that there was a problem, she asked the broker if she could meet with the potential buyer in person. In talking with him directly, she discovered that this man was worried about the large investment he would be making in the building since he was buying the condominium for his mother and for other relatives. My friend explained her experience with the building, telling him of both the positive and negative features. Her straightforward approach relaxed the buyer. Feeling that he now had a better understanding of the investment he would be making, he signed the contract and the deal was completed without any further delay.

Recently, a client, who has since become a friend, called me to suggest a technical venture with some of our products. He said that he was willing to invest his own money to hire programmers who would develop a new delivery system for our company's employment tests. After speaking about this project for a few minutes, I asked him what he hoped to accomplish in making this substantial investment. The motivation behind his proposal was that he hoped to be able to increase his client base by providing this new service. I then expressed my doubt that this plan actually would increase his client list in any significant way.

The idea that my prediction about this would be accurate stemmed from the fact that I already had done market research to see how we had convinced our best clients to start and continue using our products. We found that most of our larger and more reliable clients had come to us by word of mouth or by meeting us at a convention. They had signed on because they had received immediate personal attention from one of our staff members.

Despite the fact that my company has purchased hundreds of computers over the years, there are no answering machines or answering services used by our company during regular business hours. This is due to my strong belief that customers, as well as friends, want direct and open communication in order to feel comfortable in a relationship.

Before our best clients had purchased any large number of tests, I usually had met with them personally, either at a convention or business meeting. Sometimes, I had met with them several times over the course of a few years before they became loyal users of our products. It used to amaze me when the focus of my potential clients often was on some personal information, such as whether I knew a friend of theirs or where I had gone to college, rather than on the value and predictive validity of our products. It was the relationship we were building that was most relevant to them.

I advised my client that it was his rapport with potential users of his services that was more important than developing sophisticated delivery systems. Efficient systems already were available to do that job. I explained that we had invested several times in similar projects that had added aggravation rather than clients or revenues to our business. While a new system may or may not be of interest to some clients, this idea was bound to take my client away from his daily work. Unless the new delivery system truly was essential in order to keep up with other companies competing for the same clients, it probably would be more of a distraction than help. If my client spent that same time and money calling on new prospects, I believed that he would be more successful in expanding his customer base.

A perfect example of a successful interaction and development of a friendship in business occurred recently while I was getting ready to host a large family reunion. In the midst of the preparations for this weekend, I received a call from a salesman in a music company where I previously had purchased some musical equipment. The call was "after hours" and, before calling me, the salesman had considered whether or not to make any more calls that evening. He hit the jackpot with me. I actually had the name of his company on a list of the numbers I had planned to call as soon as I had time. Since he called me, I figured it was a good idea to go ahead and order the equipment I needed. Without having to do much more than saying hello and telling me the name of his company, this man made a large sale.

Our interaction did not end there. While talking with this salesman, I mentioned a few problems I was having in the recording process. After doing some research, he called me back with information about how to fix these problems. In our conversation, I also had mentioned something about my son living in Ithaca, New York and he remarked that his associate at work, an audio engineer, had recently moved from there. After some questioning, it turned out that his colleague had recorded the music of one of my cousins, a well-known musician in that city, and had used her band's rhythm section in his own band. Now both the salesman and I felt a new connection. We had family and friends who knew each other, which made it seem appropriate for us to become friends, too.

To continue, this salesman visited my web site and listened to some of my music. He called back to tell me how much he liked it and I told him about the problems I was having with getting my audio files to play over the Internet. He advised me that if I switched to a different type of file, my listeners could have nearly instant access to the music rather than having to wait for my current slow files to download. He gave me the name of a

31

web hosting service and some tips on how I might change my site to make it more accessible.

I never expected to obtain so much information from a "cold calling" salesman, and I usually am abrupt with telemarketers who call me at home. However, since this salesman's products were in the area of my interest and he was so personable over the phone, I was open to all possibilities. I ordered the additional equipment that he recommended, providing him with another commission. The next day, I followed up on this man's suggestions and gave my web site manager the information. Within two days, and with the help of my staff, my site was moved to a different hosting service, my audio files were available for instant listening, and problems were solved that I had expected would take a few more months to resolve.

When I received the new equipment in the mail, I was pleased with most of it, but had a problem with one part. The salesman again researched the situation and provided me with a satisfactory answer on how to fix it. A day later, I had another problem figuring out how a piece of equipment worked. He called back and that problem was fixed, too. This interaction reminded me about how we had developed some of our best customers over the years by dealing well with software incompatibility problems. Even if it took awhile to solve the technical problems, I have received dozens of compliments for having staff members willing to stay late at the office while trying to help clients with their computers. By teaming up with clients to solve their problems, vendors often can create more good will and future business than if they spend the same time sending out free products or making additional sales calls.

Since he kept complimenting me about my music, I added the salesman's name to my mailing list and sent him a copy of my newest CD. A few days later, he called back to tell me how much he had enjoyed the songs. His comments sounded like a record review, so I asked if he would write his comments so that I could put them in a reviewer's section on my revised web site.

He said that he would be happy to help me with that. He sent his review within a few days and gave me permission to use his well-known music company's name in order to identify his qualifications as well. He also made the suggestion that I send some of my stories about success in the workplace to the "e-zines," or magazines on the web that frequently are looking for new articles. He thought I could persuade more people to visit my web site using that strategy.

That same week, the new web hosting service staff solved another long-term technical problem we had encountered in the development of the site. Aside from the relief felt from solving long-term problems, it made me very happy to see that good customer service still is alive and well. In fact, the new service provided "round the clock" technical support that we used on two occasions during the first week.

So far, I had spent some money, most of which I had planned to spend with this music company anyway, and had mailed out a CD. In return, I had solved two technical problems, obtained new equipment that worked, uploaded playable files to the Internet, had some new marketing ideas, gotten a review of my CD, and had two new company contacts to help me with further music or web site-related questions. This all had started with just one phone call.

While I was negotiating these changes, I told a visiting friend about my good luck in finding two accommodating companies in one week. This friend happens to be a web site designer himself. After hearing me praise my new hosting company, he expressed doubt that the service really would help me with my web site programming problems. Taking the challenge, I called the hosting service in front of him to ask another question I had wanted to find an answer to for some time. Not only did the hosting service representative tell me what was wrong, he actually fixed it for me! My cynical friend jokingly commented that he had better retire since he could not give, and had no intention of ever providing, such extensive customer service to his own clients. His area of expertise was not in customer relations and he could not compete with people who were carefully practicing such effective techniques.

To summarize, after having the good luck of calling me at a time when I happened to need new equipment, this salesman also did his homework. He built a rapport with me, the beginning of all friendships, by asking me questions and discovering a common friend or area of interest. In this case, it was my musician cousin in Ithaca. Then he listened to what I thought I needed and helped me to determine what I *really* needed. His thorough research of the equipment gave me added confidence that when he recommended a particular item, it would be of value to me. He even went to my web site to listen to the tone and style of my vocal recordings so that he could confer with another music engineer about the best microphone for my type of voice. He succeeded in selling me a new microphone by making this extra effort.

All of these activities resulted in more sales and revenues coming to his company and, later, to him. They also assured him of a future customer who could be wooed with information that did not cost him very much to give. Within three weeks, I had passed his name to another friend who also wanted to buy some equipment. This salesman's actions and their results demonstrated how finding out more about someone else and trying to help people solve their problems whenever possible are great strategies for making friends, and money, in the workplace.

It is important to note here that business acquaintances who act like friends may or may not turn out to have the genuine interest in you that results in the development of a long-term give-and-take relationship. Of course, that is true of any new person you meet in your private life, too. Therefore, seeking to create friendships in the business world should not be viewed as a phony technique employed just to get ahead. As long as your conversations with people bring some kind of enjoyment, they are worthwhile whether or not they take place in a business setting. If they result in transactions that help both parties, all the better.

In fact, it is common interests and time together that provide the cement for most successful relationships, which may be why so many people become involved in intimate relationships with people at work. One of the complaints I have heard police chiefs make in the past when talking about the "problem" of having female police officers is that when male and female officers are paired in police cars for long hours on the same mission, they often become seriously involved with each other.

Conversely, I have seen people call someone else their friend only because they have known that person a long time and not because of that "friend" actually enriching their lives in any way. If you count behavior and not longevity, it is possible that you will question the costs and benefits of maintaining some of your current relationships that you previously have labeled as friendships.

For several years, I saw a woman in therapy because of her social phobias. She would panic whenever she was at a party or on a date and felt uncomfortable talking about herself to others, especially strangers. She had not attended college at the time, had barely passed in high school, and felt that she was uneducated and could not possibly say anything that would be interesting to others. When she began to describe her relationship with her female friends, it became clear why she was having so much difficulty changing her life for the better.

As long as she was unhappy or depressed, this woman had several people around her who would console her and tell her how sorry they were that she was having such a bad time. However, as soon as she began to socialize more, received a few promotions on her job, and had more money to buy fashionable clothes, these same friends turned on her. All of a sudden, they became more standoffish and negative. While pretending to be supportive, they would warn her to stay away from any activity that they did not participate in themselves, such as obtaining a college education. After awhile, this woman began to notice the pattern herself. She stopped seeing these friends and, for some time, did not socialize at all. However, she was able to make changes in her lifestyle that gave her more control over her future. Without having to deal with the daily negative comments from the people around her, she was able to reach her goals more quickly and with less stress.

In addition to the difficulty of defining who is a friend and who is not, it is important to realize that friends change and people can outgrow old friendships both at work and in private life. As your interests change, so do the people with whom you spend your time. Neighbors who have spent years in daily contact while raising children together may find that they have little in common once their children have grown up. Business connections change with time, too, especially as people grow older, find different careers, and, eventually, retire. For this reason, it is essential to keep friendship-making skills sharp and practiced since they always will be useful.

Making and keeping friends usually starts early in childhood, but some people never realize how to maximize the chances that they will form good friendships. Often, it is thought that friends just happen to be there and the importance of strong friendships may be underestimated until a time comes when they are needed, but are not present.

My interest in studying different aspects of positive social relationships began when my eleven year-old son had difficulties with his friends one day. That afternoon, he came home from school in a very bad mood. He claimed that some of his friends had been "mean" and he felt he didn't have *any* friends anymore. We sat at the dinner table and I asked him what he did to get new friends. He didn't have a clue and I realized that his idea was to sit around and hope that new friends would come to him. While I didn't think that this thought process was unusual for a boy in junior high school, I also noted that there had been no conscious effort on his part to start or keep friendships with his classmates.

I then tried to talk with him about what he could do about the situation. I asked if he ever had given someone a compliment on purpose or if he regularly asked his friends how they were or what they were doing. His answer was "no" on both counts. I asked if he tried to keep a positive attitude so that other people would want to spend time with him. Again, his blank stare suggested that he had never thought about these things before. In my frustration in trying to help him to learn and then to remember how to act when he was with his friends, I came up with an acronym, *CAPS*. The "C" was for "Compliment Others," "A" was for "Ask Questions," "P" was for "Be Positive," and "S" was for "Smile."

The next day, I had a few hours free before a drawing class I was taking, so I sat in a nearby restaurant and began to write a long poem about this *CAPS* idea. It was similar in style to a Dr. Seuss poem and I envisioned a *CAPS* character with a big cap on his head telling the story. When I returned home that evening and read the poem to my son, my husband suggested that I make it into a book for other children to read. After two years, I completed this project and continued my observations about how children and adults make friends.

It is interesting that one of the most frequent comments I receive after an adult has read my *CAPS* story for children is that he or she knows another *adult* who "really needs" to read this book. Usually that adult is a co-worker. Since my book is written at a second grade reading level, I usually laugh and suggest that they buy it for that person's child. I have been amazed to discover the fact that many people never give the subject of making friends a thought, despite its importance for long-term satisfaction and success in life. Yet, when the idea is presented that you can create friendships by behaving in specific ways, many people want to know exactly how this is done.

I soon found that as long as I gave teenagers or adults an excuse for reading my book, they often responded quite positively to a story that I had intended to be read only by children. In some cases, I had the impression that they were grateful to me for having reminded them of something useful in a non-threatening setting.

I was invited to read my book to several fifth grade reading classes that were taught by a friend of mine. I told this teacher that I thought the book was too young for her students, but she insisted that I come to speak with her classes anyway. After the first, somewhat rowdy class, I figured out how to make this "baby" book palatable to sophisticated fifth graders. I simply started by asking how many of these students had younger brothers, sisters, neighbors or cousins who really were annoying. Everyone in the class raised his or her hand. I then told them that I was going to show them a book they could read to these younger children to help them learn how to behave better and how to stop being so annoying.

Suddenly, I had everyone's attention. Some of the children continued staring at me after I had finished reading the book, as if they wanted to hear more tips on how to make friends. You could have heard a pin drop in this class and in the classes that followed. I decided to conduct a small research project since this is one of the ingrained habits I have developed in my years of being a psychologist. I asked the children to break into groups of five or six students and assigned each group one of the four *CAPS* letters. Each group's task was to make up a skit where a conflict or argument resulted in a positive ending because someone used the friendship technique symbolized by the group's assigned letter.

What happened next surprised me again. With the exception of one skit, the solution to every conflict the children created among themselves was brought about by an intervening adult. These children, from different ethnic backgrounds and from both middle class and working class families, apparently were

38

unaware that they had any power to resolve conflicts themselves, even though this was their specific assignment. They also had a difficult time in my next exercise that included practicing the skills of asking each other questions and giving their classmates genuine compliments. I was glad that my book had been so well received and watched as the children haggled over which students could take the two school library copies home first. They were taking them to read to their little brothers and sisters, of course.

While I was disappointed to see a high level of social immaturity in these fifth graders, I realized that this may be the reason some adults have so much difficulty getting along in the workplace. If no one teaches children even the simplest of techniques for getting along with their peers, it should not be surprising when they develop inadequate interpersonal skills in adult life. When I left the school that day, I made the decision to spend some time creating additional materials to go with the book, such as a workbook that included specific exercises. I eventually developed a full school program that would aid children in their pursuit of lasting friendships.

Looking back, I cannot say precisely how my book and this project influenced my young son's social development or sense of responsibility. However, during his last two years in high school, he organized and conducted his school's first senior jazz band, organized a team to produce the school's first video yearbook, won $3,000 for a film he created and directed for Showtime Network's Youth Video Film Festival, volunteered in a soup kitchen, and helped his high school team win the New York City Fencing Championship. Three different girls invited him to attend their proms, which he did, before winning the dubious honor of being the only student in his graduating class of 250 to receive a bear hug from his principal when he was given his diploma. Now a sophomore at Cornell University, he was elected president of the music dorm last year and vice-president of the university's Residence Hall Association this year. In any case, I doubt that making him sing the songs about friendship that accompany my book did him any lasting harm. Along the way, I hope that this program has helped some adults as well.

To implement the "C" for **"Cultivate Friends"**:

1. Ask someone you have wanted to get to know better to meet you for coffee or dinner this week.

2. Pay a genuine compliment to someone about an activity or task that the person has done well.

3. Think of someone you have not spoken with in several months and call him or her tonight. Make a specific date to get together soon.

4. Take the time during your next business conversation to learn something new about the other person's interests, hobbies or family life.

5. Next time you ask someone how he or she is doing, take the time to find out by asking a few follow-up questions.

D – DEVELOP RESPECTFUL RELATIONSHIPS WITH EVERYONE

"Don't Spit in the Pail"

As a Russian immigrant once told me, "Don't spit in the pail. You may need to drink from it later." In business, this can be translated to mean that you should treat every associate with the same respect you give to your most important clients. Some people, in both business and private life, reserve their best behavior only for those who they think have the power to give them something they want right away. However, it is not unusual for someone who is in a subordinate position one day to be promoted above those who were his or her supervisors the next day.

While working as a part-time actress in New York City, I was cast as an extra in a feature film. On the bus going to the movie's location, I happened to sit next to a young woman who had just gotten off of another bus. She had arrived in the city only a few weeks earlier to begin her acting career and was fascinated to hear how I had gotten some "walk on" parts in soap operas and television shows. Even though I was hardly the big star, I was flattered that she was so interested. It had taken me a long time to figure out how to do the New York City actor's job of visiting agents, or "pounding the pavement," and I was happy to share the information. I told her everything I knew about meeting agents and finding work in these areas and she was eager and grateful to hear what I had to say. Within six months, I bumped into her again. She had been cast in a featured role in the Broadway show, *Grease*, and, in a very short time, she had become the real expert on how to get work in New York theatre.

In the years before I used my own tests to screen potential staff members, I relied on interviews to hire employees. A woman who had traveled all over the world, and appeared to be well qualified for one of my jobs, made a good impression on me at her interview and I offered her the position. At that time, we also had some students working for the company. On this woman's second day at work, she began to inappropriately scold one of the students in front of other employees for not bringing her something she needed. Her behavior was unacceptable in other areas as well and she was asked to leave our company within a week. The same student to whom she had spoken so rudely took her place only two months later and eventually became a manager in another business. Burning bridges or "spitting in the pail" rarely pays off with anything other than bad will.

One of the most successful people I have known started out as a foreign graduate student in a large Midwestern university. Dan was my future husband's roommate and barely could communicate in broken English when we first met him. Nevertheless, he had enrolled in a master's program in journalism and spent the next two years learning the language and managing to interview every dignitary who visited the university, including the President. He asked questions constantly of everyone around him, dealt admirably with the handicap of learning English from a roommate who spoke with a thick New York City accent, and never seemed to tire in the pursuit of his goals. When he graduated, he had written more published articles in English than any of the other students in his program.

A few years later, after he returned to his country, Dan wanted to come back to work in the U.S. He had made a contact, through constant calling and follow-up, of a publisher's assistant in a large foreign magazine publishing company. This company was going to be launching an important magazine in the U.S. and already had selected its publisher in New York. If our friend wanted to get a job there, he would have to fly to New York City at his own expense to be interviewed by this publisher.

Dan stayed with us when he came to New York, but returned from his interview in an unusually depressed mood. Even though the publisher's employer had arranged for this interview, the publisher had been sarcastic and somewhat rude to our friend. Apparently annoyed with Dan for taking up his valuable time, this publisher sat back in his chair and put his feet up on his desk during the interview. He then told Dan, in no uncertain terms, that there was no job for him and that he did not see why the company needed another person who spoke both languages, since the publisher already could do that himself. Dan was crestfallen. He had taken a transatlantic flight for nothing.

Within a few weeks, however, Dan had returned to the home office and reported to his contact that the publisher had no need for his services. Then, to everyone's surprise except his own, he convinced the employer to hire him to be a "liaison" between the publisher and the employer. Dan had used the publisher's rudeness to launch a new job development strategy. He simply focused on the fact that since this publisher obviously did not want anyone with contacts in the home office to be involved with the magazine, it probably was a very good idea for someone from the employer's country to keep an eye on that American publisher!

To make a long story short, within two years, Dan was sitting in that same publisher's glass-enclosed office. This time the tables were turned, though. The magazine had not done well and it was Dan's new job to fire the publisher as part of the magazine's liquidation that he was supervising for his bosses back home. While the publisher was out of a job in this company, Dan did not relax by putting his feet up on the desk as the publisher had done. Instead, he figured out how to sell back large quantities of unused paper at a profit and managed the magazine's liquidation so well that he was given a permanent job. After this, he began a fifteen-year long career with this company that sent him around the world, first as a troubleshooter and then as the publisher of magazines in the U.S. and Asia. He ultimately became a much more powerful, and wealthy, figure in the publishing business than the man who rudely had refused to consider hiring him in the first place.

Reviewing this story, I would bet that had the first publisher ever taken one of my psychological tests, his profile would have been similar to a group of people I carefully studied after having my own problems with an employee.

After about ten years of doing what I could to build my company, I decided that it was important to hire a person who could take over my job. By training someone else to make sales and to manage some of the detailed activities in the office, I was hoping to move ahead to a more creative and interesting role. As usual, I interviewed job candidates and selected a man who had completed a graduate degree and appeared eager to work in the testing business. I also had asked him to take a new test that I had developed to measure a person's past academic performance, willingness to work, social skills, confidence and goal orientation.

I first had given this test to about fifty of my friends and family members, including the magazine publisher. Since I knew these people quite well, I was familiar with their work-related successes and failures as well as their personality strengths and weaknesses. I had questioned each person carefully whenever they answered items on this test in a way that I did not expect. By doing this, I was able to remove questions that were ambiguous or did not clearly measure what they were intended to measure. Although I had not conducted extensive validation studies yet with this instrument, I was able to review the results of my job applicants by comparing them with the results of my known sample group.

In this man's case, his test scores looked good to me. He had high scores on most of the scales, suggesting that he was hardworking, bright, and outgoing. Also, he did not have any scores that were below the average of a large group of entry-level job candidates I previously had tested.

For the first several weeks in my company, my new employee worked primarily in sales. He was very energetic and was able to bring in so many test orders over the phone from psychologists that I was amazed. I began to teach him about the business and spent several months training him in all aspects of my company. He seemed like the perfect addition to a growing business and I was happy to have someone working for me who seemed so enthusiastic. I taught him what I had learned about approaching prospective clients and we even created some new telemarketing scripts to use in making sales.

However, before this man had worked six months in the company, I began to receive a high number of returns on the orders he had obtained. The psychologists to whom he had sold test starter kits told me that they either had not made the orders or had not understood exactly what my employee was saying when he offered them a "trial" using the test starter kit. Apparently, they hadn't been told that they would be billed $40 for this product, although I had trained this employee to clearly explain the pricing as part of his presentation to customers. When I confronted him, this man made excuses and later lied about what he had told a client. Then he broke something in the office and lied to the other employees, who knew he had been the only one in the room at the time.

After several efforts to work things out with this employee, and several complaints from customers and other staff members, I finally asked him to leave. I was confused and disappointed. This man had appeared to be quite bright, sociable, and hardworking, both in his interview and on my written test. His energy level certainly had been high. He had started out well and then failed to follow-up with his assignments. He had made a positive impression, at first, and then made people angry about his "minor omissions" and outright lies. Again, here I was presenting myself as the expert psychologist and businesswoman with tests for assessing job candidates. Yet, like the plumber with a leaking faucet, I was unable to hire a staff of competent people myself!

In my frustration over this situation, I decided to review all of the profiles of the fifty family members and friends who previously had taken my test to see what I had missed. One night, after my employees had left the office, I spread the test results out over three desks to see if I could find anything different about the man I just had fired. What I found was fascinating and probably never would have come to my attention if I had not made such a large investment first in this employee.

While my employee's scores all were above average compared with those of the job candidates I had tested, there were two scores that, as a pair, were lower on his profile than the scores of all the people I knew well who were tested. What I finally noticed was that no one else had both the Candor *and* Sensitivity scores on the *Hilson Personnel Profile/Success Quotient (HPP/SQ)* below the score of 60t, the score at one standard deviation above the norm. In technical terms, these two scores still were above the average scores, but below the first standard deviation above the norm, while his other scores each were higher than one standard deviation above the norm. What mattered most to me was that no other profile spread out on the desks had this combination of scores. If a person had a Candor score under 60t, their Sensitivity score was higher than 60t and vice-versa. It turned out that this person's relatively low scores for both Candor and Sensitivity on this test identified a characteristic that was predictive of the somewhat arrogant and insensitive behavior pattern I had observed in this person.

I was glad that I had found something different on this person's test since I certainly had missed it in the interview and even in the first few weeks of his employment. To see if this difference meant something that could be applied to the evaluation of future job candidates, I called one of my most research-oriented clients. He already had tested 130 managers in his company with the *HPP/SQ* and had evaluated each profile carefully. Without telling him why I wanted the information, I asked him to check if any of his managers had both Candor and Sensitivity scores under 60t on this test.

When my client called back, he was very excited. His first comment was, "Well, you finally did it. I was waiting for you to figure out how to read these profiles!" He then proceeded to tell me that the people who had both Sensitivity *and* Candor scores under 60t were poorly performing managers who had been rated by their supervisors as unable to work well with others. They were failing at their jobs despite the fact that they each had other very positive qualities, such as strong academic ability or a willingness to work hard. Nevertheless, they also were excellent at alienating those around them, whether supervisors or subordinates, and were known as "the jerks" or worse.

Candor, as measured on the *HPP/SQ*, refers to a willingness to admit to minor shortcomings. This means that a person with a high score will admit to errors more readily than others, and in doing so, will be more open to finding ways to improve performance. The Sensitivity scale measures the degree of discomfort a person has when he or she has said something wrong or has hurt someone else's feelings. With a relatively low sensitivity score, it is less likely that the person will care if they have been boorish or insensitive. When you combine the qualities of perceived flawlessness ("I don't need anyone else's help since I am always right") and insensitivity ("and I don't really care how you feel about it"), the result is pompous behavior that matches the style and behavior pattern of my employee and the New York publisher previously described.

A few months later, this combination of test scores identified some white-collar sociopaths, including an accountant who was caught printing thousands of dollars of unauthorized checks to himself off of his company's computer. I had warned the person who had decided to hire this accountant that, even though the man appeared to be extremely bright and socially outgoing, his lack of sensitivity and candor were of great concern to me based on personal experience. It turned out that the employee was the son of a friend of the employer, so my advice was ignored. The employer eventually had to call the police and have his friend's son arrested, which was much worse than if he just had refused to hire the man in the first place.

Another employee with this profile walked off the job with no explanation at a time when her employers needed her most. In this case, I also had cautioned the employers about this woman's profile and they had decided that they would take their chances since they wanted to fill the position quickly. Instead, they spent extra money training her and had to start over with a new person anyway. While finding a subtle indicator of such difficult employees was unintended in the development of this test, it did teach me a lesson about how combinations of characteristics measured on standardized personality tests can predict performance.

While personality-related characteristics or behavior patterns are difficult to change, this is not an impossible task. Becoming aware of your own tendencies is the first step needed in order to make changes that will serve you well in the future. In my own case, a very high score on the *HPP/SQ* Sensitivity scale was clearly related to my reluctance to fire inadequately performing employees. When I began to document the job performance of my staff in a standard manner, using the same performance review forms for each employee, I learned to be less sensitive to other people's problems that I could not solve. This made it much easier for me to build a more effective and efficient staff. In noticing that good managers show high Candor scores, but do not allow the mistakes of others to reflect on them, I was able to gain better control of my business, allowing my hardworking employees to shine and the others to leave.

On the other hand, despite your best efforts to be appropriately sensitive, it is unlikely that you can work for years without annoying anyone else. Sometimes you can find a way to avoid conflicts, and, other times, you must do battle for an important principle or issue that will be certain to make you an enemy or two. However, minimizing the number of people who are antagonized by your actions is a reasonable goal. By increasing your social sensitivity quotient, without going to the other extreme of being overly accommodating, and by admitting to your shortcomings without being overly defensive, you can increase your chances of success by treating others with the same respect that you would like to receive yourself.

By working to develop respectful relationships with everyone, regardless of his or her current position, chances are maximized that your contacts will be willing to assist you in the future. In fact, some of my company's active clients were developed after employees left my business to work elsewhere and brought my tests with them to their new companies.

To implement the **"D"** for **"Develop Respectful Relationships with Everyone"**:

1. Talk to people with whom you work with the same respect that you would like to receive. Keep the idea in your head, regardless of how absurd it may seem at the time, that anyone you have contact with anywhere you go could be your employer or best customer someday.

2. Write a list of your three greatest shortcomings at work. Be honest with yourself about your relative strengths and weaknesses. Pick one area of weakness and write down three ways you will try to improve upon this shortcoming in the next month.

3. Make an effort to admit when you have made a mistake at work, even if it was not entirely your fault.

4. Start a conversation today with someone at work or in your neighborhood who you see frequently but have rarely, if ever, met socially. Write down at least two things you have learned about this person and what he or she does that you do not know how to do (e.g. speaks another language, plays soccer etc..)

E – EXERCISE, EAT WELL, & ENJOY THE SCENERY

"...It's a great art to saunter!"

...Henry David Thoreau

In recent years, the media has focused much attention on the importance of diet, exercise, and recreation for the maintenance of good health and a balanced lifestyle. It would seem that further discussion of these topics would be redundant. However, in recent years, I have noticed an increase in the number of people who are workaholics, mesmerized and held captive by new technologies. While all of the recent additions to our daily tools, such as laptop computers, cell phones, and the Internet, have made some aspects of our jobs and private lives easier, they also have spawned a new generation of workers who never stop because they always can stay connected to the outside world. I have noticed some of my friends are working longer hours than ever before just to "keep up with the competition" in their various fields.

While you are out fishing in the wilderness, you now can call home to be aggravated that your electrician still has not fixed the broken light switch in your kitchen. You also can find out that your boss has been looking for you and expects you to call within an hour no matter where you are or what you are doing. With the addition of cable television, e-mail, and electronic games, children can be left alone to stare into a screen for hours without needing adult supervision. This allows adults to spend more guilt-free time at their work. One businessman returned my phone call after taking his wife to the hairdresser. He was supposed to be on vacation, so he sneaked out to the parking lot where she wouldn't see him and used his cell phone. If you wish, you even can work off of your laptop, sending messages out all over the planet from your bathroom!

I went through a long period of being the stereotypical workaholic myself, long before the new technologies took over and captured the time and attention of my friends. The day I finally figured out that there was something wrong was when my underwear fell off.

I was working as an outside contractor for the human resources department of a government agency. Since this agency was hiring several thousand new employees each year, often testing and reviewing over one hundred new applicants each week, I would carry dozens of cases home every day. I felt that I had little time to do the laundry and no time to shop. Everything was about work.

One afternoon, I was hurrying to the subway, carrying two heavy shopping bags of files to review that night. All of a sudden, I felt my underpants slip down to my ankles in the middle of the sidewalk. This was a pair with old elastic that I had dug out to wear since I hadn't made time to do the laundry. I put the bags down, quickly stepped out of the underpants and stuffed them into one of the bags. As I successfully completed this maneuver, I looked around to see if anyone was watching. There was a man walking right behind me who was laughing so hard that he could barely contain himself. I decided it was time to slow down and treat myself to some new underwear, among other things.

I thought my underwear story was pretty extreme until I heard about one of my brother's friends, a workaholic engineer. This man was so attached to his hand-held computer, that he took it into a public bathroom stall with him one day so that he could continue working. This was in the early days of hand-held computers when the batteries on these small instruments would run out periodically. When they did, there was only a thirty-second time limit for users to change the batteries before all of the memory was lost and the information that was stored in the computer was permanently erased. Naturally, the battery died just as he was sitting in the stall.

This engineer was prepared for all contingencies, however, and had an extra set of batteries with him in his pants pocket. There was no way he could stand to lose all of the data he had put into this instrument. What he did *not* expect was that, while he was sitting in the stall, one of the batteries flew out of his hand and rolled off into another stall. With less than thirty seconds to find the battery or lose his information forever, we only can imagine what he looked like as he tore out of the stall with his pants down to crawl on his hands and knees, frantically searching for the battery in someone else's stall. All was well when he succeeded, saved his data, and gave everyone in the bathroom a shock and then a good laugh.

While many goal-oriented people have workaholic tendencies, it is the control over these tendencies that allows for increased capacity to enjoy the benefits of success. Taking time off every day to relax, ride a bike, take a walk, or just "smell the roses" is the best way to maintain balance in your life. If you have a sedentary job, just taking a ten-minute walk around the block can relieve stress that you may not realize is keeping you from doing your best work. Now that many people can do some or all of their work out of their homes, they often merge their careers with their private lives. When there are fewer boundaries, it is easier to spend much of your time with your mind on work, never being able to really get away from it all or turn off the thoughts about what you should do next. Taking breaks and time away, even if it is only for a few minutes or hours, is essential in order to maintain the mental balance that allows for the most creative and efficient work to be completed.

The importance of your immediate surroundings cannot be underestimated. A messy room tends to create anxiety for people who enter it, even if they have created the mess themselves. A person's immediate surroundings can provide inspiration for creative work or can stifle all motivation. When talking about the value of inspiring scenery, a friend of mine mentioned a talented musician he knew who was trying to make a living in Russia by writing music for a singer. This man was living and working in a small room and complained to my friend that he was having trouble writing anything for the singer. When my friend asked him why, he replied, "Because I'm looking at garbage!" Even if you think you *like* your messy office or your chaotic lifestyle, getting rid of the garbage, the mess, and the noise, even if only for a short time, can provide a tremendous boost to your morale.

Since everyone has his or her own way to relax, and one person's relaxation can be another's tension, finding your own niche in the area of relaxation is as important as finding a career that makes you happy. Whatever it is that makes you feel calm and contented, whether it is staring at a mountain, sauntering around its base, or climbing it, *that* is what you should do to reward yourself for the efforts you put into maintaining your career. Even if you love what you do for a living, time away will restore energy and increase your ability to focus on the next task.

To implement the **"E"** for **"Exercise, Eat Well, & Enjoy the Scenery"**:

1. Set at least thirty minutes aside each day to engage in the exercise activity of your choice. Ride a bike, take a walk, go for a swim, or play a game with someone else, like tennis or racquetball.

2. At least once a week, take time to leave your usual environment of home and work with the mission of finding a beautiful sight or feeling somewhere else. This can be the lights of a city or the quiet of a wooded area.

3. If you know that your usual diet is not one that would be found in any standard diet or good nutrition book within the last ten years, set one day aside each week to eat more balanced, healthy meals. Buy one of those books if you don't have one already.

F – FAVORS FOR OTHERS WILL BE RETURNED

"…Though Not Necessarily By The Same Person"

For those looking at the business world from the outside, one image is that it is a cutthroat place where the strong and ruthless triumph over those who are weak, naïve, and even kind. However, it is the relationship between people in business, as in anywhere else, that really drives commerce and the development of new products forward. The best relationships are those where the talents, skills, and even personality styles of an individual complement those of another. If one person cooks and the other one cleans, both will benefit from each other's efforts. If one person is good at coming up with new ideas and the other can put those ideas on paper so that someone else will invest in their development, a business can grow.

While the plan of working cooperatively with co-workers and clients is one that usually brings success, kindness to others in business often does not result in the expected outcome. To anticipate immediate feedback or rewards from making an effort on someone else's behalf in business or personal life frequently brings disappointment. Sometimes this leads to the unfortunate conclusion that it is not worth helping anyone else since they tend not to repay the favors. One thing I have learned from experience is that doing favors or making a special effort for one person, even when it is at his or her request, often does not lead to gaining such favors in return. However, practicing a kind and positive approach to everyone will result in positive outcomes, though ones that may be unexpected.

For example, I met a professor at a convention who was interested in using some of our tests with his students who were studying assessment techniques. I explained that these tests were used only for employment purposes and that I did not want to compromise their security by providing copies of tests to classes of students. However, since he was so insistent about wanting to use tests for this purpose, I went back to my office and my staff and I developed a new set of instruments specifically for classroom discussion and evaluation. We created a report that identified a student's strengths and weaknesses so that the person taking the test as part of a course requirement also could learn about his or her potential in different areas.

When I called the professor to tell him I had developed the test he had requested for his students, he informed me that he was glad I had worked on the project, but he was not really interested. I guess he had been playing some sort of game with me at the convention to see if I would accommodate his whim. Meanwhile, we introduced this new test to other educators and they have used the instrument in their classes. The payback was not as I expected from the professor, but we sold the new product to other clients instead.

A few years later, a similar incident occurred with the director of an engineering firm. He asked that we create a set of norms on our cognitive test so that he could compare his engineers with other engineers tested. After we had provided him with free tests and then created customized norms for him, he decided not to use the test at all. Again, this business effort did not pan out after we had spent a fair amount of time doing this project at the expense of our own and other client's needs. Nevertheless, we later were able to provide another engineering firm with these data.

I now look at all requests for customized products or special favors as opportunities to expand. As long as I do not dwell on whether or not there is a return on our initial investment of time and resources, I can maintain a positive attitude when the immediate return is not forthcoming. Surprisingly, it is usually someone completely different from the one for whom the favor is done in the first place who returns that special effort with another benefit. I do not mean to say that it is not important to analyze and try to predict which efforts may result in the largest returns. In our case, we must decide which type of tests to develop. However, it is often the smaller efforts, not considered due to the results of any market research study, that can lead to the most interesting projects, creative ideas, innovation, and expansion.

In making a continuous effort to communicate with others and freely share ideas, you never know when or where you will have a significant positive effect on someone else's life. One thing is certain. The genuine appreciation of others for something you have done is one of the most satisfying gifts you can receive.

For example, it was rewarding for me when a woman, who I had met only one time previously, approached me at a party to thank me for enriching her life. At first, I had no idea what she meant. It turned out that, in a casual conversation a year earlier, I had told her how I had learned that most people can learn to sing if they are willing to study and practice for several years. This woman always had wanted to sing and was excited to tell me that, at my suggestion, she had been taking classical voice training lessons for the past year. She had seen progress in her ability to sing that she never would have expected before talking with me. I certainly hadn't anticipated that my own experiment in learning to sing would result in helping someone else to reach a personal goal.

Another time, when a friend's father died, I immediately took a trip to my hometown to see this friend and offer some support to her family. Her family had provided me with a "home away from home" while I was growing up and I felt good that I was able to be there at this time. During our visit, my friend became quite upset at the realization that she had not done the same for me when my father had died a few years earlier. She had not understood how distressing it is to lose a parent and how important it is to have close friends around. She simply had been too busy to think about coming home. I reassured her that she shouldn't worry about this since now she would jump at the opportunity to help someone else in the same situation. I had been consoled by another girlfriend at the time and was happy to support this friend now. I was repaying the favor, even though it was to a different person.

To implement the **"F"** for **"Favors for Others Will be Returned"**:

1. Remember that kindness to others will be returned, though not necessarily from the same person.

2. Make a special effort to do a favor for someone at work this week.

3. When someone does you a favor and you do not know how to repay it, do a similar favor for someone else instead.

G – GO FOR THE GOLD

"Aim High"
... Sir Edmund Hillary

In the Broadway show, *Gypsy*, Mama Rose is the quintessential stage mother. When her daughter is about to perform on stage, this mother shrieks at the top of her lungs, "Sing out, Louise!" This line has become a half joke in our family, and we now say it whenever we want to encourage each other to "go for the gold!"

There was one time in particular when I found this kind of seemingly obnoxious coaching to be especially useful. My older daughter was about to perform in a singing recital with her teacher's other voice students and a few parents. She was supposed to sing an Italian art song that she had learned and had sung very well during her lesson earlier that day. However, just before the recital, I could see her beginning to panic. She told me that she didn't think she could sing this song and when she rehearsed a few bars with the accompanist, her voice nearly disappeared into a timid whisper-like sound.

I sat down next to her and told her that I was going to be the only one listening for her to do just one thing: hit the back wall of the concert hall with her voice and make it stand out. I told her that if she did not feel comfortable doing it for herself, then she should do it as a gift to me just for that day. I also told her that my only possible disappointment would be if she didn't try. For some reason, this worked and she "sang out" in a way that her teacher and the rest of us had never heard before. The videotape we still watch of her smiling performance that day shows my daughter's willingness to take a chance, meeting the challenge directly despite her fears of failure. After that experience, her confidence grew. Within two years, she asked me if she could participate in a singing competition and became a semi-finalist in the classical division of the 2000 *National*

Association of Teachers of Singing competition for high school students.

My daughter's willingness to throw her voice out to the back wall probably helped her to make more progress than she would have made with ten more hours of vocal exercises in the classroom. By suggesting a specific image for her to concentrate on during her performance, and telling her to think of it as a gift to me, I helped her to focus on something other than herself. Nowadays, she doesn't need much coaching in this area and enjoys singing her original pop songs with her guitar whenever there is an audience. Occasionally, though, when one of us is worried about an upcoming performance, the others shout, "Sing out, Louise!"

I may have gotten the idea to tell my daughter to hit the wall with her voice from experience in my first professional psychology position twenty years earlier. When I worked as a therapist in a phobia clinic, my job was to take groups of phobics on trips to elevators, stores, and sometimes even airplanes, so that they could practice breathing exercises to avoid panic attacks when trying to face their feared activities. In one of these groups, I was working with a claustrophobic woman who also was a very successful competitive swimmer.

Each week, after the phobic clients completed their group session, they would be given homework assignments. This might include walking down the block to a neighbor's house, going into a store, or riding an elevator. Each week, the assignments became more difficult as the clients progressively focused on their most feared situations. My claustrophobic client returned without having completed her assignments during the first few weeks. While talking with her about the idea of going into elevators in order to conquer her fear, I used her knowledge of swimming to make a point.

In competitive swimming, a good racing turn is essential in order to kick off properly from the wall and to gain additional momentum when heading towards the other side. In order to do this turn, swimmers must estimate how far they are from the wall as they are approaching it since they should start the turn before they actually touch the side of the pool. The judgment needed here requires experience. If you stop swimming to start your turn too early, you will miss the wall entirely and will have to turn around again to touch it. If you start the turn too late, you may hit or touch the wall with your body instead of with the bottom of your feet. You even could hit your head if you miscalculate your distance to the wall. However, if you have gone all the way to the wall, at least you will have a better chance of touching it and will be allowed to continue on in the race.

Using her swimming experience, I showed this woman how she always had "gone to the wall" when racing and, now, she just had to do the same thing when facing her fears. The other members of the group picked up this saying and talked about "going all the way to the wall" or "hitting the wall" or what would happen if they hit their heads on the wall, or panicked, when they faced a phobic situation. I told them that in trying to "push the envelope," or making efforts to stretch to the outermost limits possible every time, they would reach their goals faster. We frequently referred to the need to "hit the wall" or "go for the gold" whenever group members planned to practice something new, meaning that they would try to do their best every time they faced their fears. After all, it may be better to relax and do nothing than to make half-hearted efforts that are likely to fail.

Because of my two daughters' years of involvement in the sport of gymnastics, I have had the opportunity to watch gymnasts, with ability levels from beginner to national champion, practice their skills before a competition. Two girls have made a lasting impression on me with their focus and approach to their practice time. One was a college-bound high school senior who practiced in a small gym in a rural area. She was the only girl at the highest level in this gym and she practiced alone much of the time while her coaches worked with as many as forty other girls in different levels. Without thinking that anyone was watching her, she made every attempt at each apparatus as if she were competing at the Olympics. Her preparation was consistent and focused and, just watching her practice, I could understand how it was that she had been able to reach this high level in a gym that did not offer the most modern training facility or the companionship of other high-level artistic gymnasts. Her dedication was complete and she later went on to compete successfully on a college gymnastics team.

The second girl was a rhythmic gymnast and a member of the U.S. National Team. In one competition, she received the ranking of second in the country, even after accidentally spilling soda on her ribbon prior to her final routine, weighing it down and making it almost impossible to perform well. Having watched her in practice, I understood how she was able to pull off that situation with the class of a champion. Every time I watched her practice, it was the same. She, too, was focused, concentrating on her skills without allowing any distractions. It seemed that she rarely, if ever, took long breaks during practice time. Her interest was in doing the elements of her routines perfectly and she rehearsed weak sections over and over again without needing her coach to provide additional encouragement. When she was about to compete, she practiced up until the time she was called to the floor to perform. While this seemed excessive compared to the more relaxed behavior of other gymnasts, it was her routines that tended to receive the highest scores. The simple reason for this may be that, given that every person on a national team has exceptional talent, it is the ones who practice the most who are closer to automatic perfection when the pressure is on to compete.

Another characteristic of champions in many different fields is their attention to detail and to the fundamentals of whatever they are practicing. Close analysis of the details of any endeavor can bring an understanding that makes eventual mastery much easier. To be consistently successful in life, and to be recognized for excellence in professional careers, business, or management positions, long months and sometimes even decades of practice may be required. In a speech to members of his organization, the president of the American Psychological Association recently stated his opinion that becoming an expert in anything takes about twenty years. Whether finding success or reaching personal goals takes one or twenty years, it will be those who "go for the gold" who are most likely to find it.

To implement the **"G"** for **"Go for the Gold"**:

1. Next time you practice something you have been working on, imagine that this is the last time you ever will have the opportunity to do this activity. Try to do the best work you can at each attempt or practice session.

2. At your next practice session, pretend that you are the person you admire most in this area and imagine the person performing flawlessly. Visualize the transfer of your idol's ability to yourself and keep practicing until you can perform at least one element of the activity without any errors.

3. When you have mastered something for the first time, try to do it five more times before you stop your practice.

4. Before each practice or attempt to perform a skill, do warm-up exercises with the same attention and focus that you give to the full skill.

5. Work until you have made a specific improvement, even if it is a small one, each time you practice.

H – HONESTY, INTEGRITY, & ACCURACY

**"There are victories of the soul and spirit.
Sometimes, even if you lose, you win"**

...Elie Wiesel

While there are many techniques for getting what you want, satisfying long-term success will remain elusive if there is not a basic foundation of honesty, integrity, and accuracy. So many times I have heard people say, "Yeah, but look at that guy. He's got it all and that's because he's stepped on everyone else in order to get there." I can name some people today who fall into that category and seem to be doing well at the moment. Of course, there are short-term gains that can be made by taking advantage of other people or by forcing your way into a better position. However, eventually most people who do their business without integrity lose so much respect from others that, even when they pay people to work for them or pay people off to rescue them from their troubles, they cannot easily sustain their ill-gotten gains. "Scamming" others to get something for nothing is a shortcut that rarely works well as a lifelong policy.

Regardless of how upstanding a company may try to be, it does not take long before issues involving ethics and integrity require business managers to make decisions. At one time, during the late 1980's, there was a boom in the test publishing industry. The polygraph was banned by a new Federal law for use in employee selection because of its lack of validity. This meant that a large number of professional polygraphers were out of work. Many of these were retired police officers who conducted investigations and used the polygraph machine to help investigate job candidates entering the departments where they used to work. In order to stay in business, some people started companies that provided new written tests for polygraphers and salespeople to sell to agencies and private corporations that could be used instead of the polygraph for investigating the suitability of applicants.

While my company once had been one of three or four other testing companies attending trade shows in the security field, all of a sudden there were twenty or more different companies. Many of these new businesses advertised that they had the tests that would solve employer's problems. One company stated that it could predict employee violence. Another boasted of having separately scored tests for different racial groups. That type of test scoring eventually became illegal.

Still another company bragged that it was able to predict employee honesty with eighty percent accuracy. What it did not reveal was that its test was screening out more than fifty percent of the apparently honest employees in order to identify a percentage of those who were dishonest. In general, these companies had little data to back up their claims and rarely, if ever, sent representatives to psychological or academic conferences to present research. They relied upon salespeople to market their products to unsuspecting consumers in private corporations who wanted to believe that what they claimed was accurate.

The majority of consumers had no background in testing and assumed that the tests they were purchasing had been "validated" or were "reliable." This was based on literature provided by these companies that purposely confused these two very different concepts in the testing field. In some cases, companies even obtained letters from attorneys stating that their tests were "reliable," even though this is a statistical term and was not what the attorneys were qualified to discuss or able to verify.

Many of these companies eventually went out of business. However, there was a time when they seemed to take over the industry and I was afraid that they would take over our customers as well. At a trade show, one company's owner came over to me and, very seriously, asked me how he should go about conducting validation studies on his test. In the psychological testing field, these studies are supposed to be completed before a test is offered for sale. In fact, I had spent five years making

65

sure that my first psychological test was predictive of job performance. However, this business already was selling its test to clients from an expensive booth in the exhibit hall with no research at all. As more savvy consumers had started asking for data to prove that his test actually worked, this business owner was looking for a quick way to keep up with the competition. Having a proven product only mattered to him when his untested questionnaire was challenged. Shocked that he had the nerve to ask me such a question, I tried not to be sarcastic as I suggested that he try to find someone who knew about statistics to conduct a few studies.

Eventually, some of the marketing hype presented by companies that was not based on reliable research results was exposed in a Federal government report. This did not happen, however, until thousands of unvalidated tests had been purchased and used by unsuspecting clients. The government report also did not stop the use of these tests in the marketplace. This was a difficult time for my company and we had to constantly educate test users about realistic research results in this area and about the difference between tests with predictive studies and tests without such information. I even published an article entitled *"The Seven Deadly Sins or Little White Lies of Honesty Test Vendors"* in three different journals and trade papers. This article enraged the owners of some of these companies and I made a few enemies. However, we did survive as a business while several of the other companies eventually stopped selling their poorly developed, though slickly marketed, products.

I experienced other very difficult times in business when I became entangled in a few situations involving corruption in government agencies. In one case, it appeared that business owners were paying corrupt government employees to gain contracts illegally. Apparently, I was "getting in their way" by bidding for contracts with high-level professional services. One night, a mid-level government employee made a phone call to my home at 11 P.M. His purpose was to tell me that I should hire some of his "people" so that they could "help" me keep my contract. When I refused and "blew the whistle" about this incident and other related problems to the appropriate government authority, it turned out that the top official in this department was part of the corruption ring himself. I was threatened or "warned" to walk away from the problem, my home was broken into in retaliation, two of my contracts were terminated without any opportunity to bid on them, and the government investigation that had started with my information was somehow terminated.

When I tried to explain what was going on to a member of the local media, he did not find the information about rigged contracts dramatic or compelling enough and declined to research the story. After some additional unsuccessful attempts to correct this situation, I finally sent out a message that I no longer would bid on new government contracts in that community. At first, it seemed that unscrupulous individuals were getting away with building personal wealth using illegal means and, in some cases, this had been going on for years. However, three years later, these activities became the focus of a public scandal. For months, the people who had caused me so much trouble made headlines as newspaper articles and television news shows identified them as corrupt officials.

During the next ten years, I was aware that my business suffered due to corruption in two other government agencies. In different places in the country, the "bad guys," who took advantage of the weaknesses in their organizations, eventually ended up in the newspapers. They were exposed to the public as their numerous misdeeds no longer were tolerated by honest employees or by other people who saw what they were doing. Whenever this happened, I was pleased to see how staying honest, though not always bringing quick riches, was by far the best path to follow in the long run.

I also have watched two brothers develop different lifestyles as adults. Scamming and scheming to "get rich quick" became a way of life for one of them. He increased his income by making false insurance claims and participating in pyramid schemes. However, it was his brother, who worked in a legitimate business for less money, at first, who ended up with the most security and peace of mind. When this brother finally bought himself a beautiful home, he was pleased that he had earned every penny of his investment honestly. Whether on a business or personal level, being honest and accurate is a sure way to be able to look into the mirror proudly at what you have accomplished.

To implement the **"H"** for **"Honesty, Integrity, & Accuracy"**:

1. Assess the general level of integrity of the people with whom you spend your time. Are you proud of them or do they do things on a regular basis that you would not like to be associated with if their activities were made public?

2. As you make new friends, try to determine if their approach to life is one that will be compatible with yours. Surround yourself with friends whose standards for integrity and accuracy are the same or higher than your own standards.

3. Make a resolution to provide honest and accurate information to others whether you are selling a house, going on a blind date, or marketing a product.

I – INTENSE CONCENTRATION BRINGS RESULTS

**"Success is to be measured not as much by the position
that one has reached in life as by the obstacles which
one has overcome to succeed"**

... Booker T. Washington

When people are in trouble or find themselves in extreme circumstances, amazing things often happen. What seems impossible becomes reality and, all of a sudden, people's abilities rise up to fit their needs. What is it that allows for a parent to lift a car off of a child after an accident? How do some ordinary people manage to survive for days after becoming lost in the wilderness? Is it a miraculous survival instinct or simply a matter of intense concentration and unbridled energy that produces such extraordinary results?

There have been several times in my life when I've noticed people's ability to conquer the seemingly unconquerable through sheer willpower and determination. It might be obvious that the person who can concentrate for the time necessary to complete a task is the one who is able to complete that task successfully. However, many failures may be due to a lack of concentration in general.

After a number of incidents, when I found myself able to succeed at a new skill under pressure, I realized how we all have a much greater capacity for success and competence than we might think. It is not uncommon for lecturers to begin their motivational speeches with the comment that we use only one tenth or less of our full brainpower most of the time. Although that may be hard to prove, it does seem that we put a percentage of our competencies on hold, waiting for the right time to test ourselves.

One afternoon, I was visiting a high school friend whose father had a boat. Her mother hated boating but had come along for the day's excursion at a lake. Unfortunately, there was something wrong with the boat's motor and we sat around the dock for two hours in the heat while my friend's father tried to fix it. We were in a remote location and there were no other people around. As we began to boil in the sun, my friend's mother became more and more agitated and angry about being there at all. She was complaining bitterly and I felt uncomfortable as this family's tension mounted.

Finally, I decided to try to see what was the matter. I got up from where my friend and her mother were sitting and went over to see what the father was doing. He was covered with sweat and tools were scattered all over the ground. It was hot and I really wanted to go out on the water myself. With determination and unusual concentration, I listened intently to my friend's father as he explained the mechanical problem. I figured that he must be desperate to tell me the details at all. Trying to be a good student, I examined the motor with him, never having looked at a boat's motor before, and tried to understand what he was telling me. On a regular day, I would have let this technical information pass right over my head. In fact, on a regular day, I never would have asked in the first place. However, I was so hot and uncomfortable that I was determined to get out of this situation and to help solve the problem.

After carefully studying the motor, I made a suggestion and it worked. Within a half hour, we were out on the water having the Sunday afternoon we had planned. Everyone was amazed, especially me, that I had been able to come up with a workable solution. Looking back, I now realize that I had concentrated so intently on the problem that, even though I am not mechanically inclined, it became solvable. I wondered about how it was that I could fix something right away that a *father*, the supposedly mechanical one, couldn't figure out. That day helped me to believe in my own untapped potential for solving problems, even in an area I previously thought was reserved for men. It may be that a few of these kind of experiences gave me the courage to face challenges when I later started my business in the male-dominated fields of law enforcement and security.

A few years later, I attended college and was working at the local YMCA as a swimming instructor of three and four year old toddlers. The job was indoors and I asked the director if he had any job possibilities for the summer that might allow me to work outdoors. He told me that he was planning to purchase a fourteen-foot sailboat to use for sailing instruction on the nearby lake. He was going to hire two people to teach and had already hired one of them. Without realizing how difficult sailing is, because I had never done it, I told him, "Oh, yes. I can do that!" He told me that I would have to become certified by the American Red Cross as a sailing instructor first, but then the job was mine.

During my spring break, I signed up for a five-day basic sailing course. It was then that I discovered the fact that sailing is a skill requiring a great deal of knowledge of boat parts, wind direction, and strategy. It takes a long time for most people to learn how to sail a boat well, not to mention learning how to teach sailing to others. Obviously, my boss at the YMCA had never sailed himself. I was under a bit of pressure as I realized that I had five days to learn everything before taking the Red Cross certification course in a few weeks. I had only one opportunity to learn, since if I failed the certification course, I would not be able to take the job. The thought of working in a smelly indoor pool with screaming toddlers all summer was excellent motivation for this new learning.

With intense concentration, I listened to the dry land lectures about techniques and boat parts. I wrote everything down in a large notebook, including the jokes told by the instructor so that I could use them later. Luckily for me, he was an excellent teacher and, within five days, I had transcribed the full sailing course that must have taken the sailing school a long time to develop.

It was one thing to take careful notes and to listen in a classroom. I had been doing this, or pretending to do this, in classrooms all of my life. However, going on a sailboat and figuring out where the wind was blowing, the first important task for a good sailor to master, was quite another issue. I remember feeling the wind coming from all directions when the instructor said that we must find the wind's direction and learn to sail according to its constantly changing position in relation to the boat.

At first, I panicked. I am not a natural with anything involving directions. In fact, this is one area where I have a history of problems. Even though I often was near the top of my class in academic subjects, I was the lowest scorer on a map reading and direction skills test in elementary school. I have since become lost at least sixty percent of the time when I drive anywhere. I have the dubious distinction of having driven to the wrong town and, once, I even flew to the wrong city. In mid-air, on my way to a convention, I realized that my plane was heading for Louisville, Kentucky and I had meant to fly to Lexington! I received a very strange look from the stewardess when I asked her to confirm the flight's destination.

When I passed my driver's test after the second attempt, my friends laughed at me whenever I tried to drive them somewhere. I was pathetic. I couldn't even find my way to the one parking lot of the one movie theatre on the one main street in the small city I grew up in all of my life. My children now tell endless stories of my driving escapades, including the time I drove around Kennedy Airport for forty-five minutes, unable to find the exit.

Since the skill of sailing involves spatial reasoning, navigation, and boat direction, it was especially challenging for me. After feeling the stress of initial panic, I thought to myself, "You do not have the time to be a dumb girl here. Pay attention and figure this out or you will be stuck in that hot and smelly basement pool with the babies all summer."

This was a great challenge for me and I remember concentrating in a way that I had never done before. Despite a strong natural inclination *against* learning this skill, I concentrated so hard that I was able to break through a major mental barrier. Even though my efforts at journeying to unknown places today still are best served by a guide who can figure out directions for me, I was able to find my way on the sailboat. I concentrated more intently than I ever had done in the classroom and insisted to myself that I could *do* this.

With full use of the power of concentration, I figured out where the wind's direction was on the first day out on the sailboat. Since paying such keen attention to a task that would normally be quite difficult for me, I learned it so well that I have never had any trouble with it since. I immediately became a good sailor because I wanted it so much, and I was able to captain a 24-foot sloop sailing upwind in 28-knot winds for twelve miles without an instructor on board at the end of four days of instruction. I also was lucky that, being a beginner, I did not know enough to be scared about the rough weather.

In unusual circumstances, our instructors' motorboat broke and they failed to warn me, and the other students in my boat, to head back to port due to dangerous conditions. Instead, I took the helm and sailed the boat upwind all the way to a port I had never been to before that day. What I thought must be normal ocean sailing turned out to be a major tropical storm that was about to hit the area. While out in the ocean's channel, I also innocently conducted a fairly insane "man overboard" drill to successfully rescue another student's hat that had blown overboard into the two to three foot waves. When I brought the sailboat safely to the dock after completing this journey, the instructors were jumping up and down with such relief that one actually fell in the water. No beginners from their school had ever been out in such dangerous weather, with or without an instructor, and they had worried about whether we would make it or if our surviving relatives would sue them for years in court.

Much later, after I had taught over two hundred people how to sail, including college professors and mechanics, I found out how rare it is for someone to learn about the wind so quickly. Maybe one person in every thirty or forty students catches on to this concept within the first few times out on a sailboat. To be able to captain a small boat in heavy winds in such a short time was a feat I accomplished only because of sheer willpower and mental concentration, with a bit of dumb luck.

I surprised myself a third time, several years later on the first day of my first professional job working as a psychologist in a hospital. I felt fortunate that I was able to get a ride from a psychiatrist, Carol, who lived nearby. I did not own a car at the time and public transportation to the hospital would have taken at least two hours. On the highway, about thirty minutes from the hospital, we had a flat tire. It was a very chilly autumn day as we got out of the car, both standing helplessly by the road. Carol wondered how she could find a way to call the *American Automobile Association* for help. This was before the age of car phones or cell phones and there were no phone booths or exits nearby.

As I stood there, I thought about how the first official patient of my career was scheduled to see me in a half hour in the phobia clinic. I thought about how this person had finally gotten the courage to face her fears and now I would miss her appointment. The screening session would have to be cancelled, since there were no other psychologists coming in to work until later in the day. Knowing how difficult it can be for phobic individuals to talk about their problems, I worried about the effort that this person may have expended to get herself to her first clinic appointment that morning. Of course, I also worried about the impression I would make walking in an hour or two late for my first day at a new job.

All things considered, I decided that we didn't have time to wait the several hours it would take to find a phone, call someone, have them drive in rush hour traffic to find us, and then change the tire. Since it was rush hour and we were in city traffic, no one was stopping voluntarily to help us either. I asked Carol to open the trunk and told her that I wanted to try to change the tire myself. She was shocked, but seemed amenable. I had watched my father change a flat tire once, so I had a vague idea of how it should be done. I studied the jack that did not come with instructions, opened it up, and was determined that I would get it to work.

Somehow, with willpower and intense concentration, I figured out how to put the jack under the tire and began to change the tire myself. I wasn't strong enough to get the lug nuts off using the tire iron alone, so I enlisted Carol's help. We pulled on the tire iron together and each nut eventually came off. Within a few minutes, I had changed the tire and let the jack down. I was filthy. My gloves were in shreds, my coat was covered with grease and dirt, and I was shivering in the cold. However, we were driving on the road again and I arrived at the clinic door only five or ten minutes late.

My patient was waiting and I was exhilarated. I washed my hands and face, laughed at how I looked in the mirror, and started a nine-year career at the hospital. If someone had told me earlier that morning that I would have to change a flat tire out on the highway in order to get to work, I would have laughed and told them that it would be impossible. However, my determination to get to work on time led to the concentration necessary for me to figure out how to succeed at a new task.

When people feel that there is urgency, they can stretch themselves to reach new limits. My father was a nuclear physicist who taught me, literally, how to live life fully right up until the last breath. During his last days, he was determined to finish the solution to a mathematical problem that some young professors wanted him to explain for an article on one of their research projects. He had not finished the work when I found him bedridden for the first time during his three-year illness. I asked him what he wanted to do and he told me that he wanted to finish the paper. I said that we could do it together and helped him up from his bed.

In the chair in his den, he typed the rest of the paper. When he had finished, he was having difficulty seeing the computer screen, so I looked at the equations for him. I didn't have a clue what the work was about, but I noticed that there was a closing parenthesis missing at the end of one of the mathematical formulas. He agreed that he had made a mistake, and told me exactly what I should type in order to fix it. Then he was satisfied that the work was complete and he asked to go back to bed. He told me that it was my job now to print out the article and mail it in the morning. I had a feeling that he was not doing well and I knew he wanted to know that the paper was printed and mailed.

Of course, his old printer wasn't working properly and it was too late to call anyone or go to a store to replace it. I couldn't get the paper set up so that it would feed through the printer and felt badly that I couldn't do the task my dad had assigned. Again, with intense concentration, I was determined to get it to function. I focused on slowly moving some small parts of the machinery, fiddling with them while trying all possible ways they could move, and practically willed them to work. I managed to get my father's last paper printed that night and showed it to him in the morning, with the stamps and address on the envelope. He was pleased. After some brief conversation and loving words, he died a few hours later.

While I have used my own stories of focus, positive determination, and willpower to illustrate my point, they are not unique. Everyone has the capacity to do great and extraordinary things as well as slightly difficult things in life if opportunities are approached with an open mind and a bit of optimism.

To implement the **"I"** for **"Intense Concentration Brings Results"**:

1. Find a task that you never have done before. Concentrate for thirty minutes on learning how to do it properly. Practice the skill at least two or three times each week.

2. Find the instruction manual for a piece of equipment you frequently use (that effort, in itself, may be an extraordinary feat). Then read the first four pages of the instruction manual carefully. Write down what you have learned about the equipment that you didn't know before you read the manual.

3. Increase your powers of intense concentration each day, starting with five minutes and moving up to thirty. Direct your attention to the task you are doing, but focus more intently than usual on each detail of that task before you do it.

J – JUSTIFY NEGATIVE EXPERIENCES BY MAKING THEM GOOD

"When You Get A Lemon, Make Lemonade"

Sometimes it is easy to become "stuck" on what we perceive to be our so-called "failures." In business, this can be the "failure" to get the right position, the "failure" to hold it, the "failure" to understand the new accounting system, or the "failure" to sell products to a potential customer. In management, it can be the "failure" to complete team projects on time, the "failure" to foresee how a competitor's products affect the marketplace, or the "failure" to motivate staff. Whatever the failure may be, those who seem to keep "getting it all" do not have any fewer failures on their list. What they may have that is different, though, are innovative ways to turn those failures into successes.

The first step is to realize that failure alone is not necessarily a bad thing. If you are a poor driver and keep failing your driver's test, the extra time you take to learn to drive correctly may seem inconvenient, but also may save your life. Although finding the "silver lining" in negative experiences may seem like a rationalization, this is exactly what perpetual winners do best.

Also, what seems like a failure today actually may lead to a larger success tomorrow. A good example of this for me was when I lost a large contract with a law enforcement department where I had worked as a private direct services provider for several years. When I lost my contract to "in-house" psychologists from another agency who had convinced my department to merge its recruitment and personnel services with that agency's services, I was demoralized. I had created a model program for selection, even published articles about it, and now "my" department was going back to a set of procedures that I knew were not as efficient or effective as the ones I had developed. Although the reasons for losing the contract were political, I wondered what I could have done, if anything, to change the situation. I also worried about how I would cover all of the expenses of my business in the future.

Despite my disappointment, I soon realized that I no longer needed to spend hours of my time in meetings and "schmoozing" with administrators in local agencies. In fact, I now had the opportunity, due to my "failure" to keep my contract with this one agency, to make contact with other psychologists who provided these same services to agencies throughout the country.

I made a conscious decision to attempt to avoid the politics of individual organizations in the future. After I decided that I would let local psychologists deal with the day-to-day negotiations involved with law enforcement agencies, I made an important change in the direction of my business. I no longer wrote lengthy proposals to individual agencies, but, rather, helped other psychologists to do this and to propose the use of my tests in their programs. I built a brand-new business over the next few years that no longer depended upon local politics.

My "failure" had given me the opportunity to have a greater success in another area of business. I often have thought how *unfortunate* it would have been if I actually had retained that contract. I would have been so busy managing the daily workload that I never would have had time to diversify and to create a business that now depends on good products rather than on my hourly work.

A second situation that initially appeared to be a major blow to my business occurred when a test owned by one company, but licensed to my company for distribution, was then given to another company with an exclusive distribution contract. Since nearly half the income of my business came from this test, I was *sure* that we could not survive. Nonetheless, the time I spent calling customers and making contact with them about the fact that I could no longer provide this test merely strengthened my relationship with these customers. Many of them simply stopped using the test in question and eventually added more of our company's tests to their programs. In fact, the tests they added might not have been developed if we hadn't lost the distribution rights to the other company's test in the first place!

The situation that made it most clear to me that "failures" or losses in business can lead to greater successes occurred when new laws affecting psychological testing were passed, including the Americans with Disabilities Act. Here, I lobbied long and hard to explain why police officer testing should be made an exception to this law. I believed that law enforcement agencies should be allowed to ask questions about substance abuse and mental disabilities prior to making a conditional job offer, as is now prohibited by this law. I had conducted research that showed how important these questions were in predicting a police officer's job performance and knew that agencies would end up spending significant amounts of money completing background investigations on people who would later fail the psychological evaluation if there were no exception granted. I lost this battle and believed that my "failure" again would have a very negative impact on my business.

It is true that psychologists no longer can test or interview candidates at the early stages of employee selection. It also is true that they are not as involved in the overall process as they were in the past. Some of my most predictive tests cannot be given until a bona fide conditional offer of employment has been made to a job candidate. However, as an alternative, I have been able to develop new instruments that do not ask the legally forbidden questions. Now these new tests can be used at the initial recruitment stage by human resources departments and background investigation sections of all organizations, including law enforcement agencies.

I also have developed an instrument scoring and delivery system that can benefit the psychologists even though they cannot be involved in the interpretation of these early-stage questionnaires. By identifying candidates who are most likely to fail later on in the selection process or on the job, my company now assists organizations with appropriate questionnaires that are not nearly as costly as comprehensive background investigations. Even though psychologists cannot be involved in this process at the early stages, I was able to find a way to make this potential "failure" a success.

So many times, what seems to be a great loss, at first, simply becomes another opportunity for individual growth. In my personal life, I can think of several examples.

For instance, I lost my first election when I ran for the office of student council vice-president at the age of thirteen. I was embarrassed that I hadn't been as clever as the girl who won. She had started her speech with "Dear A students, B students, C students, D students... and Friends" and the whole school had laughed for what seemed like hours to me. Without a good joke, and knowing that I probably would blow the punch line even if I *did* have one, I felt my chances for winning that election slipping away.

I lost a second time when I ran for the same student council office again in high school. This time, I lost to the school's basketball star. I still hadn't learned my lesson since my idealistic, and very *boring,* speech was about changing the election process so that the council's members would be more representative of the student body. My opponent's speech was about a decorating theme for the senior prom and having soda machines in the lunchroom. The following year, I applied what I had learned about the need to appeal to your audience and finally won an election when I ran for a different office.

What is most interesting about this now is the way I approached that second election. I was determined to "have fun" running for office and told myself the night before the election that, this time, if I lost, I wouldn't worry about it. I didn't. I already was practicing how to lose gracefully, how to try again, and how to hold my head high even if I was feeling low. Being able to do these things in business is invaluable and I later was grateful that I had the opportunity to learn these lessons at a young age.

A year later, I was put on the "waiting list" at the college of my choice and was not accepted there for my freshman year. At that time, I saw this as a major failure. However, I met my future husband on the first day of class at a different university I attended the next year. We both eventually transferred to and graduated from my first choice university. My detour to a different school was not without its benefits and I appreciated the first choice school even more when I finally got there.

These stories continued throughout our adult lives including the time, years later, when we bid on a house that we really wanted that would have required extensive repairs and restoration work. We were very disappointed when the broker's boss arranged for the house to be sold to a couple who had put in a bid after ours that was more than the asking price. However, less than six months later, we found and bought our dream house that needed no repairs. If we had been able to purchase the first house, we probably still would be working on it!

One of the most difficult times in my life came when I became critically ill three and a half years ago. As I was recovering from pneumonia, after spending three weeks on a respirator, my doctors found a large blood vessel tumor that had fractured my vertebrae and was compressing my spinal cord. To eradicate the excruciating pain and threat of imminent paralysis from this tumor, I faced an experimental research procedure at the National Institutes of Health that had been conducted on only eight other people before me.

After waiting through weeks of pain until the doctors felt that I was strong enough to withstand the treatment, it was successful. Almost miraculously, the tumor was reduced to a non-threatening size and my spinal cord was normal again.

However, I was left to deal with the constant pain that resulted from the tumor and lasted for another three years.

It was much more difficult to find something positive that could come from this experience, but while I was dealing with it, I was determined to find a way back into my life. I did two things that helped me to justify the bad times and to make something good come from them.

First, I decided that I would do everything possible to lead a normal existence despite my disability. I was told that I could not lift anything over five pounds for at least six months. In fact, after the procedure, it hurt to lift a small handbag. While in the hospital, I was told that my younger daughter had qualified to compete in her first national rhythmic gymnastics competition to be held in California. People thought I was crazy when I said, from my hospital bed in New York, that I would be there. A month later, with the help of a good friend in California who carried my handbag and drove me around, I was able to attend that competition.

My daughter turned eleven on that weekend and was the star of the two-day event. In a field of forty-eight competitors, she was in first place after three of four required routines and had won a gold medal for her rope routine. Coaches from all over the country were watching her and offered their congratulations in the hotel hallways. My daughter's coach was very excited and expected her to win the All-Around gold medal at the end of the second day. Unfortunately, during the final element of the final routine, my daughter failed to catch her last toss of the hoop. After this mistake, she moved down to fourth place All-Around and her coach was devastated.

I had a different reaction. At lunch, the coach looked at me and asked, "Are you *really* happy about this?" I answered, "Yes. How could I be anything but happy? Here we are. My daughter has done a great job and has a pocketful of medals. I was able to watch her looking so graceful and beautiful out there on the floor. She's only eleven years old and we're sitting here in California having a wonderful lunch, celebrating life. I didn't expect to be here at all, so this time can't be anything but good!"

When the coach saw how a different perspective could change the entire view of the competition's outcome, she relaxed and we all enjoyed ourselves for the rest of the trip. Despite the pain, I was determined to enjoy the good things in life. Through that lunchtime conversation, I believe that I helped my daughter to see how you can choose to focus on the positive even when others see only the negative aspects of a situation.

In fact, just missing the All-Around medal in that competition may have helped my daughter to learn the lesson of perseverance. She continued to practice rhythmic gymnastics at our local community center, moved up a few levels, and qualified for the 2000 U.S. Junior Olympics three years later. We flew to Seattle, where she helped her team win the team competition gold medal and she won the individual gold medal for her floor routine. I believe that my daughter enjoyed winning that medal more than any other since she had made a great personal effort in order to qualify for the competition. I also had noticed her determination when, the week before the meet, she chose to spend several hours of her free time carefully sewing sequins onto one of her costumes.

Now that she was a little older, she appreciated what it meant to be participating at such a high level in her sport, with or without medals. As I proudly watched her step up on the podium to receive her award, I remembered what a gardener had once advised me about a newly planted hedge, "Be patient. The trees will grow!"

The second thing I did to help in my recovery from trauma was to think about how I could find a way to make something positive and long lasting come from my experiences. I was scheduled to give a lecture at a conference a month later that usually consisted of dry statistics relating to predicting law enforcement officer behavior from psychological tests. For years, I had given these lectures, bringing new research but focusing on academic themes.

I decided to go to this conference and give a different kind of lecture, one that would be more personal, yet still helpful to my psychologist friends. Since many of them often work with traumatized police officers after critical events, such as shootings, I thought that it would be useful to share the thoughts of a psychologist going through trauma herself. In order to do this in a twenty-minute time slot, I wanted to be well organized.

While taking one of my rehabilitative walks with my husband, I brought along a small pad of paper and a pencil. During that walk, I jotted down all of the ideas that were helping me return to a healthy mental and physical state. Then I put them together using the alphabet to anchor the main points. My lecture was a success and I was encouraged to use it as the outline for a self-help book on how to recover from trauma. When I later gave copies of this book, *ABC's for Inner Strength & Well-Being*, to the dozens of people who had helped me during my illness, I felt good that I was able to show my appreciation for their support by giving them something in return.

A few years later, a colleague called to ask me for another copy of my book. He had given his copy to a friend and now was facing a major illness himself. He remembered how useful my book had been to his friend and wanted to review what I had written, even though he was a psychologist and already knew the major points I had covered. I was pleased that I could help him at such a stressful time in his life and felt that the time I had spent writing the book was well worth the effort.

While traumatic experiences never can be "justified," I did see how some good could come from them. Like Tom Sawyer, who watched his Aunt Polly grieve and then attended his own funeral, I had the somewhat surreal experience of greeting over

85

fifty people who came into my hospital room or called me after I was breathing on my own again. One by one, they described their reactions and initial grief when they thought that I might die on the respirator. I didn't know that I could have such a strong effect on others. The support and love I received from so many people at that time is something wonderful that I never will forget.

One of my friends, a physician, recently donated a part of his liver to try to save his ailing sister. Tragically, she did not survive the operation. Like my own experience, my friend and his wife were touched, in a way they described as "life-altering," by the outpouring of emotional support they received.

Of course, we all would like to be exempt from two of the things we share, our fallibility and mortality. Nevertheless, learning to accept and to better cope with them can bring a freedom of spirit that transcends the ordinary. By writing my book on trauma, I now have a permanent reminder of what I learned from a difficult time in my life and am content that I have been able to help others in similar situations.

Whether circumstances help to make a bad experience better or you actively create new solutions to problems, most failures can lead to new successes if you guide them there.

To implement the "J" for **"Justify Negative Experiences and Make Them Good"**:

1. Think of three times when you have been disappointed and thought that you failed at something important. Reanalyze your failures by writing down the lessons you learned from these experiences.

2. List ten failures or setbacks in your business and/or personal life and figure out how many of them actually led to something good in the end.

3. Make a resolution to evaluate failures as "future successes in the making" as you determine what you would do differently, if anything, the next time.

4. Tell others about mistakes you have made when they have problems similar to your own. Conversely, listen carefully when people share their mistakes and important "lessons of life" with you.

K – KEEP A FOCUS ON DISCOVERY & GROWTH

"Have Faith and Pursue the Unknown End"

...Oliver Wendell Holmes, Jr.

In order to "have it all," you first have to discover exactly what "it all" is! For most people, there are a number of exciting things to do in the world that are quite personally satisfying but may take awhile to discover. By keeping an open mind and allowing yourself to explore new areas, trying each one with a full effort, you can find activities you truly will enjoy and eliminate those that just sound good in theory.

One friend, who I hadn't seen in several years, described his adventures to me on a recent visit. He had tried a few new things and discovered more about himself in the process. First, he had decided that it would be fun to build his own small sailboat. He found a do-it-yourself ad for a kit that would allow him to build a fifteen-foot ketch and ordered it through the mail.

When the kit came, he struggled to lug the heavy pieces into his garage. For many months, he labored to put this boat together. After spending more hours than he ever intended, he finished the work and wondered why anyone would spend so much time doing this kind of activity. Even though it was satisfying to have put a boat together himself, the effort, for him, was too great. If he ever needed another boat, he would let someone else do that work.

This same friend also admitted that he always had wanted to become a pilot. After years of working at his career, he finally decided that it was time to take flying lessons. He took the required lessons and passed the basic course and tests needed to earn his small plane pilot's license. Along the way, he discovered that his concept of how it would be to pilot his own plane did not match up with reality.

My friend initially thought that he would sit at the controls and would be able to relax and enjoy the scenery. What he discovered is that flying even small planes requires frequent communication with other people through the headphones that pilots wear. Since this communication is done at the same radio frequency for all pilots in the area, even when you are not talking with an air traffic controller yourself, you hear a near-constant stream of dialogue and other noise coming through your headphones. Also, you have to listen carefully to what is being said, especially when you are near an airport, since you may receive important information or a specific direction at any time.

My friend, who prefers solitude to social events with strangers, found his flying experience to be challenging and interesting, but also quite stressful and uncomfortable. He described how the cockpit of small planes can become unpleasantly warm in the summertime and how the requirements of being strapped into a small seat with a tight set of headphones over his ears did not quite turn out to match his original concept of being able to "fly like a bird!" Although flying time or boat-building experiences did not turn out to be everything he had hoped they would be, he did succeed in learning new skills. By satisfying a life-long dream to pilot an airplane, and finding out which activities weren't as enjoyable for him as he had imagined, he could move on to different hobbies that would better suit his tastes.

Even if some new activities do not fully meet your expectations, they can be stepping-stones to other pursuits that will be more fulfilling. For example, I always had the fantasy of becoming a painter in my later years. On my fortieth birthday, I visited an art museum full of beautiful impressionist paintings. I realized, upon looking at them, that it probably would take years for me to learn how to paint. If I wanted to enjoy this hobby in the future, I decided that it would be a good idea to start learning how to do it now. I went home and signed up for a basic drawing class that met once a week. This led to more classes and the illustration of my children's book with simple cartoon-like drawings.

While I enjoyed the lessons and experience of drawing, I also learned my limitations. I was not particularly adept at drawing what I wanted to draw and was quite easily frustrated when my hand wasn't able to create a picture to match what my eyes were seeing. I knew that, like everything else, practice makes perfect. However, if I really wanted to reach my goal of being able to enjoy my own work, I would have to spend more time than I wanted to spend on this hobby.

Although I did not discover a true passion for making art, my efforts in learning to draw eventually led to the discovery of a talent and passion I never knew I possessed. After a friend saw my children's book, he suggested that it would be a nice story to put to music. I shrugged and said that, although I had studied piano as a child, I really didn't know anything about how to write songs. Since this man was a guitarist and once had written and directed songs for a children's musical production, he offered to write a few songs to go with my book. We shook hands on the idea and went our separate ways.

As soon as I returned home that afternoon, I began to hear music in my head that had both melody and words. I sat at my desk and started writing the lyrics on scrap paper. I wrote notes above these words like "do", "re", "mi" to remember the melody and included arrows to show whether the melody went up or down over each word. Although I wasn't thinking of this at the time, I actually was using a musical skill called "solfege" that I had learned in required elementary and junior high school music classes. It had taken over thirty years before I had any use for this knowledge, but on this day, I wanted to thank all of the music teachers who had made us learn how to read song melodies from a page of music.

In a few hours time, I had completed the theme song to go with my book and had started two additional songs whose goal

90

was to help children remember the most important ways to make friends, the subject of my book. I'll never forget how surprised I was at myself that day since I had no idea that I ever could write music. Compared to my art classes, where I had labored so hard to get the lines just right, the music seemed to flow out of my head effortlessly. I had discovered a talent and new love directly from a hobby that had not been nearly as satisfying.

It is important to remind yourself that in order to "have it all," which is actually having different things at different times, you always must be willing to learn and practice new tricks. I once overheard a beautiful young art student lamenting before class that she was turning twenty-one the next day and was just "too old." I laughed and asked what I should think of myself, being twice her age and still taking the introductory course. Her comment reminded me of when I was twenty-one and had been in a play with an actress who had just turned twenty-four. I had stared at her for a while during one of her scenes, just thinking about her age and how it must feel to be as old as twenty-four. Now I can talk with someone her age and almost forget how long it has been since I was that old. The point is that no matter what your age happens to be, you will feel young and stay on the most productive track if you constantly seek out new experiences and keep an open mind.

There are many elderly people nowadays who set wonderful examples for those in the younger generation. More people are living well into their eighties or older with decent health and several careers and hobbies under their belts. Now there is a good possibility that additional decades of active living will become the norm. One of my mother's friends, an ocean sailor hobbyist who is now eighty-three, told me that the best years of his life so far were between seventy-five and eighty. He was very serious as he explained that he had learned the most about himself and had the most fun during this time period in his life.

I also have had the benefit of watching my seventy-six year-old mother tap dance in a performance with others from her weekly class as part of a large public event. Having seen both of my parents ski racing into their seventies has stopped me from whining that I must be "too old" to be doing whatever it is I want to do. By keeping a focus on discovery and growth throughout our lives, we can avoid becoming the dog that is "too old to learn new tricks!"

To implement the **"K"** for **"Keep a Focus on Discovery and Growth"**:

1. Make a list of the recreational activities and/or hobbies you have enjoyed in your life so far. Try to pinpoint which aspect you enjoyed most about those activities.

2. Write a list of three new hobbies you think would be fun to try that would fit with or involve using the best parts of your personality.

3. Sign up for at least three classes in a subject that you never have studied before.

4. Make a habit of cutting out news articles about elderly people who are doing exciting things with their lives.

5. Write the article that you would like to see printed about you and your activities ten years from now.

6. Pick a hobby or activity that you once enjoyed doing, but have since stopped, and try it again.

L – LOOK TO CUT LOSSES, THEN TRY, TRY AGAIN

"..Know when to hold 'em, know when to fold 'em, know when to walk away, and know when to run.."

… "The Gambler" by Don Schlitz

In order to win most of the time, it is essential to know when to cut your losses. No one can win every game or every contest in life and trying to fight a losing battle often wastes scarce resources. In business and management, knowing when to walk away and start over is as important as knowing how to devise a new product or develop a new client. Along the same lines, knowing which battles to pick and which issues to leave alone can save you precious time in your efforts to stay on a positive and purposeful track.

While it is difficult to know exactly when the time has come to stop spending energy on a lost cause, keeping an eye on each project with this possibility in mind is very helpful. When I was busy building my company, I hired several people to work in the office. Since I often was away giving lectures or attending conventions, I depended upon members of my staff to do their work and maintain services for our clients without daily supervision. This non-management style only works when employees have a built-in sense of work ethic and drive to do a good job regardless of who is watching at the moment.

One year, when I was particularly busy, I hired three employees who did not do their jobs. This was when I had developed some pre-employment tests for law enforcement candidates but had not yet developed screening tools for general employees in corporate settings. I had not given either personality or aptitude tests to anyone on my staff. It was ironic that I had employees without work ethic and my entire business was based on the idea that I could develop tests to screen out job candidates who would not perform well!

Whenever I was in the office, I noticed that work was not being finished as fast as I had hoped. Mistakes were being made every day on procedures that had been well documented in easy-to-understand manuals. Since these staff members always were very pleasant and polite with me, I did not understand what was wrong. Knowing how busy I was, I figured that I was having these problems because I didn't have time to work closely enough with my staff. I also believed that it was my fault that the work wasn't being done quickly because I hadn't personally shown my employees how to complete each procedure more efficiently.

It turned out that when I was away, one of my female employees would visit a bar at lunchtime, coming back to the office unable to function. Unbeknownst to me, another woman actually brought a blanket with her to work and took daily naps on the floor. A third employee apparently spent much of his time using the telephone for personal calls. Meanwhile, I had been praising them for work that was completed and had tried to be satisfied with whatever amount of work they managed to do in a week.

I only discovered the gravity of this situation when I hired someone who did have a strong work ethic and was horrified at what he saw going on behind my back. Once I understood that people were taking advantage of their freedom at work, I was unsure of what to do about it. I went to a convention and was fortunate to speak with an experienced businessman there who gave me invaluable advice. When I described what was happening in my office, he talked to me about percentages.

He explained his theory of cutting losses in the following manner. He thought that although every new employee may have only a fifty-fifty chance of failing, the employee who is already failing is a certain problem. Therefore, at least there is a fifty percent chance that a new person will do a better job. He suggested that I find a good reason either to lay off or fire each and every employee who was not doing acceptable work, even if it meant having a limited staff for awhile. I thought that this would be a drastic step, but I listened. I began to document the mistakes that had been made and what those mistakes cost the company in dollars and lost time.

One day, the woman who spent her lunchtime in bars failed to arrive at a convention exhibit because, as she explained, "It was too slippery outside." This left me short-handed for a full day at a very important annual event. I finally was annoyed enough to take action.

I spent the night worrying about what I would say and how I would go about firing these employees. I was afraid of their reactions and, although I knew that they were the ones who had failed, I felt guilty about any part I may have played in their failures. There was a part of me that believed I had not provided enough guidance, challenge, or consistency as a manager.

The next day, I arrived at my office and called these employees into the room, one after the other. I held a list of the things they each had done that had hurt the company and were not up to the standards I expected. When I told the first person that his work performance was unacceptable and that he could not continue working for my company, he shrugged, nonchalantly, and said, "OK." When I fired the second employee, her reaction really shocked me. She just stared at me as if to ask, "What took you so long?" The third employee was a bit upset, but didn't say a word in her own defense. I had expected arguments, crying, something that would tell me that I was unfair and awful to have fired three employees at the same time. Instead, they quietly left my office, took their blankets, flasks, and other personal belongings out of their work areas, and left my company for good.

I realized that I had waited a very long time to change my staff and that my businessman friend had given me good advice. I began to use new tests that I developed specifically to help me select better employees. These instruments included questions about work ethic, social sensitivity, and drive. From that point on, I found that even if one person did not work out well, I did not have to deal with a group of employees again that took such liberties at work.

Cutting losses with products that are not of interest to clients, despite their interest to me, has been a more difficult task. For example, a few years ago, we developed a series of tests for teenagers to find out about antisocial or violent behavior patterns before they result in trouble or arrests. Since no other tests were available in this area, and both the media and psychologists had expressed great interest in the idea, I had invested in the development of these products. In the testing field, it takes about five years to conduct appropriate research studies to demonstrate that any new instruments are "reliable," meaning that people answer the questions in a consistent way, and "valid," meaning that the tests actually measure what they claim to measure.

For several years, during the 1980's, we gave away hundreds of these new tests for adolescents to junior and senior high schools around the country and conducted a number of statistical studies. We found some interesting results. There was a small, but significant, percentage of teenagers who admitted to having violent impulses, such as active suicidal thoughts or violent behavior patterns towards siblings. There were others who admitted to problems that no one knew about before they answered the questionnaire.

In one hospital clinic, several professionals from different disciplines, including psychologists and social workers, had evaluated a shy eleven-year old girl who looked like she was only nine. They could not determine why she was having so many adjustment difficulties at home and at school. When she took this test, now called the *Hilson Adolescent Profile (HAP)*, she endorsed an item admitting that she recently had been pregnant. This came as a surprise to everyone who knew her and the hospital's director thanked me for providing an opportunity for teenagers to admit to their problems without having to tell someone directly.

We also found that the adolescents who answered our questionnaires, after becoming involved with the juvenile justice system due to criminal activities, fell into three distinct categories. Some were antisocial without showing any remorse, the sociopathic types for whom therapeutic interventions would have limited effects, while others showed antisocial behavior patterns with personality and emotional problems that were amenable to professional intervention. Some admitted to depression, others to fears and phobias. The third group of troubled teens showed a different profile, one without the usual evidence of psychopathology or serious emotional adjustment disorders. These adolescents showed significant family problems alone, suggesting the power of the immediate environment to shape behavior. Again, I was excited about the idea that we could help administrators assess which teens would benefit most from different treatments and that we could do this in an efficient and inexpensive way.

After the data were analyzed and we were satisfied with the results, we made these tests available to school psychologists and to other professionals who work with teenagers. We had different forms of the inventory so that longer or shorter evaluations could be conducted. Despite the interesting research results, our excitement about being able to help troubled teenagers, and the resources that I had devoted to launching this new set of testing products, the project failed dismally.

It came as a shock to me that, although there had been a great deal of lip service about how important it was to help adolescents, there actually was a very strong tendency on the part of school administrators to ignore the developing problems of teenagers. When I pressed them for an explanation, I was told that they really did not want to know what was going on with their students because, if they found out about a problem, they might be legally responsible if they did not take some kind of action. The claim that schools did not have the resources to "take action" seemed rather feeble to me, but I heard this concern on more than one occasion.

Legal experts later advised me that the rationale for not implementing testing programs, as suggested by these administrators, was incorrect according to the law. Apparently, administrators and guardians of teenagers are more liable for lawsuits if they don't try to find out what is going on with those they supervise than if they find out and lack the resources to intervene. Regardless of this fact, none of this mattered. Children and teenagers don't vote or have financial clout in this country. Therefore, we were providing a luxury item, and one that seemed to have the power to open Pandora's box, rather than one that had obvious benefits for juvenile justice administrations or schools.

When other test companies developed behavioral instruments for teenagers that followed my lead, they, too, admitted that they found a similar reluctance to use these kinds of evaluation tools. Unfortunately, experienced juvenile justice administrators, who were talking with me about the changing population of young detainees back in the mid-1980's, had their predictions come true when school shootings and other violent behavior increased in the 1990's. While these behaviors often were reported as if they were a surprise to the media, the trend was not a surprise to professionals working in the field. They already had seen the growing number of teens who showed little or no remorse for their serious crimes. I felt even more strongly that better assessment and prevention programs could have helped those teenagers who were most likely to benefit from appropriate interventions.

However, I also realized that it might be time to cut our losses, and redirect our time to developing products that would have more perceived value to our clients, when I tried to give the adolescent test to a large city school system. A research director in this school system's central office was impressed with our statistical studies. She managed a large program with over thirty school psychologists in the system. After inviting me to give a presentation about the tests, she informed me that the psychologists actually had been threatened by the power they saw in the instruments. One of them even told her that it didn't seem "right" that a test could identify so many problem areas when it was the psychologist's *job* to do the same thing. My idea had been that once problems were identified, the psychologist's *job* was to do something about them!

In any case, I offered free and unlimited computer scoring of my tests for the entire school system. The only fee would be the cost of the test materials that were printed by another company. I wanted to find some way that my test could be used and had offered to dedicate one of our computers for the exclusive scoring of this school system's profiles. For several years, I saw the school system's research director at the annual psychology convention. She invited me to make additional presentations, but then, sheepishly, explained each time that she was powerless to act on my free offer. There were too many politics and too many people who felt that their turf might be invaded by a product I had developed with the idea of helping young people in trouble.

A few years later, that same school system's security division director contacted me. With the increased fighting and vandalism that was going on inside of the schools, this director wanted to buy tests that would screen the increasing number of security officers who were hired to stop the students from hurting or killing each other. There were plenty of funds and resources available to spend on hiring new officers, but not on the students themselves! The security division had no idea that I had spent so much time trying to give away tests for use in their schools. The irony of this situation was not lost on me as I finally realized the futility of trying to fight "the system." My offer of free testing still stands, though, and my company will extend it to the first school system that would like to try a preventative program rather than relying on the usual crisis management approach.

I have experienced similar frustrations when consulting with businesses and organizations that refuse to consider a proactive style of management. Like the school system I described, some managers take the position of waiting until there is a lawsuit rather than developing programs to help employees deal with problems at an early stage. On more than one occasion, I have suggested a more thorough screening or counseling program using specialized self-development tests and reports. While I never have expected that every business or organization we talk with will decide to use our products, I always am surprised when I hear the response, "If we have a problem, that's what our lawyers are for!" There is a great deal of money being spent by companies after they have an incident with a violent employee that could be used in a much more productive manner.

In any case, I have learned the importance of changing direction and refocusing goals when it becomes clear that there is little chance of succeeding in a given area. By watching for the "writing on the wall," setting specific limits, and cutting your losses sooner rather than later, negative results from poor investments of time and money can be minimized.

This works at home as well. I recently watched as some friends tried to motivate their daughter either to get a job or to go back to school. She had dropped out of school and was living at home, happy to stay in child-adult limbo as her parents paid the rent. No amount of discussion or outside counseling seemed to change the situation. When the parents tried a different approach and set a specific time for her to move out, their daughter responded by re-enrolling in school.

To implement the "L" for "**Look to Cut Losses, Then Try, Try Again**":

1. List all of the projects or programs that you currently are managing at work or at home. Check how many of these have set limits for expansion or termination.

2. List the three current or future projects that are most important to you. Write a specific plan for when you will expand those programs and when you will refocus your energy.

3. Analyze a past situation when you did not "cut your losses" in a timely manner. Write what you will do differently next time.

M – MOTIVATE OTHERS TO HELP YOU

"Lead Others as You Would Have Others Lead You"

The ability to instill excitement in other people to do something that helps you is a skill practiced by the most effective managers and world leaders. While there are coercive methods, these usually do not last for the long-term since unhappy followers eventually are bound to rebel. There are several positive ways to motivate people and each successful manager has his or her own style. However, I have noticed three common techniques used by effective leaders that are particularly useful.

The first involves always doing your best so that others will view your enthusiasm and hard work as a model and look for ways to help you. Sometimes, people find ways to help without even being asked, just because they are so inspired by high energy, competence, and a positive disposition.

My friend, Sue, is a very dedicated high school math teacher. Her husband's company transferred him to a new city and, when they moved, my friend worried that she might not find another teaching position. She began working as a substitute teacher for six months, hoping a position would open and that she could apply for a full-time job. One day, she went into a new classroom where the students were working on a subject she had taught in her old school. The regular teacher had not left any lesson plans, but Sue told the class that she would go ahead and teach the subject the way she had taught her own students in the past. She easily could have sat down at the desk and told the class to do some problems in their workbooks during that period. Instead, she asked them to tell her what they were working on and picked up where the regular teacher had left off. As usual, Sue did her best to use any time she was in a classroom to the students' advantage.

The next day, she was substituting again in the same school and the head of the math department came up to her in the lunchroom, saying that he had to talk with her. For a minute, she panicked, wondering what she had done wrong in the short time she had been working at this school. The department chairman then explained that, unbeknownst to her, one of the students in her class the day before happened to be the son of the assistant superintendent of the school system. This student had been so impressed with my friend's teaching skills and obvious dedication to teaching regardless of her position, that he had gone home and told his father that he absolutely must find a way to hire her as a full-time math teacher in the school.

Sue was offered a part-time job immediately and the administrator apologized for not being able to offer her a full time job right away. Apparently, she had too much experience to be hired at the lowest salary level, though she quickly agreed to accept the lower salary in order to work in a regular position. Since the teacher's union would not accept that idea, and other administrators preferred to hire a younger and less experienced teacher at a lower salary, my friend had to wait until the following year to secure her full-time job. It was clear that, had it not been for this unusual circumstance, it would have been extremely difficult for Sue to enter this particular job market. She was thrilled to be given the part-time position so quickly, due solely to her admirable habit of always trying her best, wherever she was, to motivate students and help them to learn the subject of math. By showing initiative and doing her job so well, she unwittingly motivated a teenage boy with a watchful eye and a powerful father to help her.

The second technique that is useful in motivating others is to ask those you supervise to do things only if you are willing to do them yourself. The best management approach is to try every job yourself for awhile, unless you are not qualified to do it, to make sure that it actually can be done the way you want it to be done. Having realistic expectations for the people who work for you is crucial for the success of any group.

One of my earliest jobs was to teach swimming to young children. I always got into the pool and showed the children how to put their faces in the water to blow bubbles. One day, I was amazed to watch a teacher trying to show students this idea without doing it herself. The students were staring at her while she talked about putting their faces in the water and blowing out air. However, when they tried to do it, only one child out of the eight students was successful. I knew that it would be a lot easier if this teacher would jump into the water and show them. Being too lazy to do this, she was unsuccessful in her teaching mission. She did manage to stay dry, though, which may have been her personal mission for that day.

Perhaps one of the most difficult things to do is to motivate others voluntarily to put their lives on the line for an outside cause. How, then, do military leaders manage to do this in times of war? I recently had the privilege of reading the unpublished memoirs and letters of an eighty-one year old neighbor who fought in both World War II and in the Korean War. His story demonstrates better than any business-related example how a person can motivate others through his own behavior. In this case, my friend's insistence upon doing everything himself that he asked his soldiers to do enabled most of them to return home safely after the war. I have included several excerpts from his letters here because his management of himself and others, in his own words, presents my view of the perfect example of a good, and effective, motivator.

Joe was the fourth of five surviving children, the son of a hard working barber during the years of the depression. He joined the Army in 1941 and worked his way up to becoming a platoon sergeant in his second tour of duty during the Korean War. Although an animation artist by trade, he was assigned to psychological warfare in a unit that set up loudspeakers in different positions between the enemy and the American front lines, known as "no man's land." His unit's job also was to check to see if the loudspeakers worked and then to set them up in another location after broadcasting audiotapes that were designed to convince the enemy to surrender.

In his memoirs, he wrote, "After being in Korea for a couple of months, I was unhappy with the way we were trained to put the speakers out in no man's land. We would crawl out on our hands and knees holding on to a guide line in the pitch dark that went by the mine fields that our troops had put out for our protection. We would try to aim the speaker into the valley where the enemy was dug in. One day at the war room, I said I thought I could do it a better way. They said, as platoon sergeant, I could try anything. The lieutenant and I went up to a position after lunch. In broad daylight, I took a speaker and crawled out well able to see where I was going and located a well hidden location, aiming the speaker exactly where I wanted it to hit. I was well covered by the infantry and a tank.

My opinion was that they would not fire artillery or mortar at one person in no man's land. Ammunition was too valuable to waste on one man. I was right, although they did fire small weapons at me. At that distance, I could see the rounds hit close by, but even if they had hit me, it would not do any serious damage. From that day on, all of my teams did the same. We never had a mishap that way. We also became more effective with our speakers. My only thought was to save us from accidentally setting off one of our own mines and probably killing or wounding one of us. I was not trying to be a hero. I loved life as much as anyone and I was determined to get back to my family in one piece."

The men in this unit worked seven days a week from six to twelve hours each day, getting their food from any troops they were with at the time. Joe made a point never to set up these loudspeakers in a location where he would feel uncomfortable staying at the post himself. He often stayed on the post with his men, even though this was not required of him as a sergeant. He wrote letters home about how it was so cold at the front that his food was frozen at times. In making a personal rule that he would not ask people to do what he was not willing to do himself, he protected the lives of those in his unit. Unfortunately, other military bosses cared more about their careers than about the lives of their men.

On June 25, 1953, Joe wrote about this incident in his letter to his wife: "I had a terrible spat with my lieutenant today about the position he chose for one of our teams while we were in the war room. I always pick spots that are not too vulnerable to enemy fire. The only way to get to this position was in an armored vehicle and it would always come under fire. I told the lieutenant that he and I must put the equipment out and spend the first night of broadcast on the position. He didn't like the idea but I made it obvious that if he didn't do it, I wouldn't consider him much of a leader. He reluctantly went with me. When we got back, I told him I thought we would rue the day we put them out there." On June 28th, Joe wrote again: "I don't know if it's getting in the papers, but the enemy is trying to prove something even at the cost of many lives. Someone must be saying special prayers for me as I have had so many close calls. For instance, one day, I was at the front with some VIP's when they started a heavy barrage right at the position we were at. We were in a heavy bunker made up of twelve by twelve beams and loaded with sand bags. By this time, I knew the pattern of fire. The shells were about the same size as our 250 m.m. Howitzer. They had fired several rounds over us and some right in front of us. I yelled to all the guys at the position that they were zeroing in directly at us. I can't tell why, but I told all of them to get out of the bunker and run for foxholes, which we all did. We scattered all over and the next hit was directly on the bunker we had just vacated. The whole thing caved in. I don't know if any of us would have been killed, but I'm sure we would have had many casualties. There have been many such close calls and I do believe it's the strength of prayer that is saving me."

In a letter he sent home to his wife on July 5, Joe wrote, "I'm heading back up to the front but I'm taking most of my gear because I have a lot of catch up work to do so I'll stay up on the front line. Right now it's pouring rain and we are not allowed to have tops on our jeeps for security reasons, so naturally, we get soaked. Seems the boys are having trouble setting up programs, so I'll help them get started. It may be a week or more, but I won't leave until I'm sure they can handle it...The more I see here, the more I get disgusted with the way things are run, like rationing ammunition and telling us when to fire and when to move forward or backward."

On July 8th, Joe wrote: "Today I was packing up the new speaker equipment in my jeep to take out to the listening post when Barry stopped me and insisted he would take the stuff himself with the two interpreters and he would do the broadcast. We had a little friendly tug-of-war and he still insisted that I was too tired and deserved a break. Before I had gotten here, I had delivered two speakers to two other positions and I had to agree that Barry was right. Besides, he said he could do a better job on the enemy with his M-1 rifle than I could with my Carbine and my Webley revolver. I told him that if anything were to break out, his orders are to take what equipment he could and get the hell out. I told him he is Signal Corps, not infantry. With that, he drove off to the listening post where he would transfer everything to the armored vehicle and out to the broadcast position."

On July 10th, Joe wrote home again: "The Chinese attacked full force, over-running the whole area. Three men and myself were pinned down in our small bunker right under their noses by small arms and mortar and hand grenades. We could hear yelling in Chinese and English. The four of us prayed out loud and, I believe, our prayers were heard. At daybreak, suddenly the flap on the bunker swung open and we fully expected to see Chinese. There stood an American lieutenant with a machine gun in his hands. He was flabbergasted. He couldn't believe that the enemy hadn't killed us. We came out to see a scene that will live in our minds forever. Everywhere we looked were bodies and wounded, both Chinese and American. The smell of gun powder mixed with the dampness from all the rain and

Graves Registration putting bodies in black bags made for a true nightmare. It wasn't over yet because medics were trying to save whoever they could, not only our own, but the enemy as well. We wandered around trying to be of some help, but now I had to get to my work.

It was my responsibility as platoon sergeant to find my speaker team. I managed to get to the spot where Barry and the two interpreters were last seen. I met one of the boys who was on the hill and I asked him if he saw Barry. He said yes, and that Barry, realizing that there was no way to get out, had stayed and fought it out with his M-1. He was hit by mortar and this guy was sure that he was dead. While at the position, I checked out all the wounded and dead bodies for Barry. I was looking mostly for his dog tags, which would have proved for sure that he was dead. I also went to Graves Registration and checked every body and parts of bodies to try to find some definite proof of his death. I had no luck.

I then called my lieutenant back at our command post to make my report. He had the nerve to ask me if they had gotten the broadcast in before we were over-run by the enemy. I told him in no uncertain terms what I thought of him and I would have more to say when I next saw him."

In August, 1953, Joe wrote: "The other day, I wrote a letter to the boy's mother. We still can't report him as killed in action, so we still list him as missing. I didn't have to write this letter, but I felt I wanted to. I told her how I felt about his being missing and that I was the last person to speak with him when he left our bunker. I told her he was a good soldier and a fine young man. She wrote and thanked me for the letter and asked me to write again. I think when I get home, I will try to see his parents."

At the end of August, 1953, Joe left the front lines for the last time. He was recognized for his bravery and leadership by being presented with a meritorious award, a medal for "valor under enemy fire" from the U.S. Army. By taking responsibility for his actions and going beyond the minimum requirements for doing his job, Joe handled tragedy with leadership and grace. When he returned home, Joe and his wife raised a family of three children that now has grown to include nine grandchildren. However, he never has forgotten the man who took his place at the front lines.

It is true that power-hungry bosses can undermine a person's good efforts. However, Joe's insistence on joining in the work of his unit, regardless of his lieutenant's attitude, resulted in the initiation of safer procedures, a life-saving anticipation of imminent danger in the bunker, and the loyalty of Joe's soldiers that ultimately saved his life. While the tragedy of war cannot be underestimated, and stakes are not as high in most business or management jobs, the characteristics of an effective leader who can motivate others to listen and act on his or her behalf remain the same.

The third skill that often is well developed in people who are excellent at motivating others is that of delegating tasks, as well as decision making, whenever possible. In order to grow from a one-person operation or department into an efficient company or group, it is necessary to practice giving up some of the control over your project or business decisions. This is true whether you work in a large or small organization. If managers insist on hovering over every detail, "micromanaging" each procedure, they will drive the people crazy who they wish to motivate to work for them. Also, many employees worry that they must be doing something wrong or that their bosses don't trust them when they are over managed.

With too much direction and supervision, employees soon lose their sense of independence or autonomy that is essential for everyone in order to maintain a feeling of well-being. Regardless of the age of a person, it is a lot easier to inspire others to do something if they believe they have some choice in at least some aspect of the situation. For example, you will receive much more cooperation from a child when you ask him to choose which of two shirts to put on, or which of two vegetables should be made for dinner tonight, than if the decision is made for him.

I recently met a woman who owns a baking business. She has worked out of her home for the past fifteen years, baking pies and delivering them herself to local stores. She said that she was tired and would like to slow down at this point. When I asked if she had anyone helping her, she replied that the only person she really could count on was herself. She commented that she only has one young helper come in after school to do some packaging on a part-time basis. She stated that she did not want other people doing the work since she would rather be the one for people to complain to if there was a mistake. She also always wanted to be the one to receive the compliments when she had done a good job. Of course, as a business owner or manager, the compliments and complaints stop at the top regardless of how many employees are involved in the process.

This woman's comments reminded me of a major mistake I made myself as an entry-level entrepreneur. In the early days, I, too, wanted to do everything myself. I enjoyed the process of learning how to create tests, conduct research, advertise, lecture, design trade show exhibits, go to meetings, and collapse at the end of each full day. I was doing the work of several people at once, and, much later, it did take three people to cover the jobs I was doing myself.

However, those three people could do my jobs and more without collapsing and they also could bring in new ideas about how the work could be done more efficiently. In other words, they could help the business grow in a way that one person, no matter how skilled or hard working, could never do alone. It took me a long time to realize that my idea of doing it all myself, with a few part-time employees, was really just a rationalization. It was my way of maintaining control so that I could feel powerful and exhausted at the same time. It was true that I would reap all of the benefits. However, the cost would be great and I would have very little time to enjoy those benefits.

I realized how flawed my reasoning was when I had the opportunity to take a close look at the personality styles of more successful entrepreneurs. I already had noticed that I was working at a more frantic pace than other business owners, all males, who seemed to buy and sell businesses in my general field with ease and profit. I was focusing on most of the details of my company and tended to become involved in nearly every project of the business. I hired people who were not qualified to take over the jobs I had created for myself and felt that, without my active participation, my company would fall apart.

In 1988, seven years before William Goleman popularized the concept of "emotional intelligence" in his book on this subject, I had developed and published information about my *"Success Quotient Theory,"* a theory that proposes that success comes from a combination of characteristics including work ethic, social skills, goal orientation, as well as academic ability. I also had developed my test, the *HPP/SQ*, that measured personality characteristics such as work ethic, drive, and social skills. In this test, I included a scale about the tendency to procrastinate. In order to see how the scales worked, I brought copies of the test to a convention where there would be many successful business owners and managers.

I asked people who stopped by our exhibit at this convention to take the test in return for a free evaluation of their results. As part of this exercise, I asked for anonymous information about salary levels, company size, and other details that would give me some idea of exactly how successful these business owners and managers had been in their companies. After looking at the profiles, I talked with several of these people, mostly males, who had done extremely well and were making far better strides in growing their businesses than I had made in growing mine.

One man, in particular, made a lasting impression. He had built a business that had been included in the *Inc. Magazine* list of the fastest growing businesses in the United States. His business was bringing in millions of dollars and his personality profile also was vastly different from my own. His score indicating a tendency to procrastinate was much higher than mine and his social sensitivity score was much lower. I was fascinated to see this profile and interviewed him on the spot to see how these scales reflected our different behavior patterns.

In the course of our conversation, I discovered that he believed his success was based on his ability to delegate responsibilities to people who were more qualified than he was to meet the various challenges of his business. His high Candor scale score suggested that he was able to admit to his own shortcomings and had good insight about his abilities relative to those of others. When I asked if he tended to procrastinate, he laughed, saying, "Oh yes. That's why I make sure to surround myself with very detail-oriented people. That's how I get so much done. I delegate everything and then go on to the next problem or project."

At that time, I actually was shocked by his comments since I always thought that I should become involved in every project in a more detailed way. I realized that while this man was involved with his employees and their projects, he was not doing the detailed work himself. There is a big difference between demonstrating a job in order to show others how it can be done, starting them on a reasonable path, and doing it all yourself. I made a vow to amend my own style and to concentrate more on learning to demonstrate and then delegate tasks to others.

I also learned from this man that to be a successful manager, it is important to be honest with yourself about your own shortcomings and yet not to be overly sensitive or always trying to "fix" other people's problems. My own scores on social sensitivity were quite high compared to others, reflecting my tendency to try to keep everyone happy around me at work,

112

regardless of the situation. I often thought that when an employee wasn't doing well at his or her job, it was my fault for not being a better boss. I realized that, like me, this man was an extrovert and was very socially oriented. He was candid about his shortcomings and intent on his goals. However, the big difference between us was that he did not let other people's problems stop him from pursuing his goals. When an employee wasn't doing well, he carefully evaluated the situation and then was comfortable in making the decision to find only the best people for the job to surround him. After seeing this man's profile, I later noticed this pattern whenever I tested a highly successful manager.

I also noticed that many women, perhaps because of how they are raised to be peacemakers in the family, are overly sensitive to social situations and may be reluctant to discipline others for fear of being disliked. In one research study, I found that females were being terminated from the job of correction officer at a much higher rate than were males from the same job. In contrast, the males had a higher number of disciplinary actions and negative reports in their records. I immediately concluded that this must be because of the "old boy's" network in this organization.

My theory was that the male bosses were more comfortable disciplining other males and may have avoided confrontations with poorly performing female employees until it was too late. My theory expanded to include the idea that the male supervisors probably did not like dealing with women who might cry if they were formally disciplined. This would mean that males were being given more opportunities from their male supervisors to correct their behavior before the situation ended with them being fired from the job. Unfortunately, I soon discovered that my brilliant theory was totally wrong. I found out that the managers of the women were mostly females while the male managers supervised the male employees in this organization.

Then I realized that it was my test's Sensitivity scale scores that made the difference. Female managers tend to score higher on this scale than males and, like me, initially may be more reluctant to give negative feedback to others. In any case, I have found that many effective managers have the combination of scores indicating a willingness to admit to their own shortcomings along with average, not high, scores on social sensitivity.

In summary, developing the skills of a good motivator includes putting forth your best effort and maintaining the balance of becoming involved in the jobs of employees as a model and leader without doing the jobs for them. While some people may do this more naturally than others, due to their inborn personality styles, this does not mean that the habits of successful motivators cannot be learned. By becoming aware of your own shortcomings and working with them, you can enhance your skills and improve results.

Finally, it is important to remember that people are motivated by more than money. In becoming a role model by approaching each job with enthusiasm, and letting those you manage know how their efforts will contribute to the goals of your organization, you will go a long way towards building an effective team.

To implement the **"M"** for **"Motivate Others to Help You"**:

1. Catch yourself practicing a skill alone when you are not giving your best effort. Change your attitude to one where each attempt is with your best effort every time whether or not anyone else is watching.

2. Teach someone a new skill by demonstrating how it is done yourself in a step-by-step manner. Practice your demonstration before you do it.

3. Select a task that you usually do yourself. Delegate that job to someone else after you have given the person some training. Then practice the art of leaving the person alone. Set a time to check progress after the task has been completed.

4. Monitor yourself so that you approach your work with enthusiasm, making sure to tell people exactly how their work will make a contribution to the end result. Always add your thanks and words of appreciation at the end so that they will want to help you again.

N – NEGOTIATE FOR 'WIN-WIN' SOLUTIONS

"The Woods are Full of Them"

... Alexander Wilson

Finding solutions to problems that will make both you and others happy is one of the most challenging tasks in business and personal life. It also is an excellent way to make friends and keep them. What is one person's pleasure often is another's pain. In a competitive environment, whether it be mating or selling commodities, the option of finding a comfortable solution for everyone frequently is overlooked in favor of the "I win, you lose" mentality. While animal instincts for survival and continuation of the species may dictate that winning at all costs in some situations is critical, carrying this concept into modern daily life as a standard often does not lead to the most satisfying solutions.

For instance, there are several individual sports that are highly competitive, are played by having participants regularly face their opponents, and require an "I win, you lose" ending. In these sports, such as tennis, fencing, and boxing, the most successful athletes must develop a very thick skin and aggressive attitude where their opponents are concerned. Sometimes, these competitors transfer an apparently belligerent attitude as well as a communication style of direct and immediately aggressive confrontation into the outside world because it is such an ingrained habit to try to "crush the opposition." There is a seemingly endless stream of news stories about previously celebrated athletes who later are arrested for violent behavior in their private lives. These crimes may result from their inappropriate reliance on intimidation and aggression rather than negotiation skills in their interactions with others.

Some self-development and leadership training programs devote a large percentage of time towards demonstrating how to break the thinking that results in combat rather than negotiation. Creative games involving two teams supposedly opposing each other result in lessons teaching how both teams will lose if they do not develop moderate solutions that help everyone. The idea is to cultivate acceptance of a solution where "I lose a little, you lose a little, but I also win something and you win something too." The goal of successful business negotiations is to have each party leave the table feeling that they have triumphed, even if the solution is not clearly in favor of one side or the other.

The problem with feuding in the modern world, aside from any physical destruction that can result, is that, in many cases, it is only the lawyers who eventually walk away with the spoils. The ability of individual competing parties to negotiate depends upon the integrity and good faith of each party. Just as a couple is doomed to failure if one of the two people really is not interested in maintaining the relationship, any conflict in business will end with negative results unless a decision maker on each side of that conflict keeps the "win-win" solution in mind at all times. Most conflicts require creative ideas to make everyone happy and it can take some time to develop these ideas. Meanwhile, tempers need to be controlled, which is easier said than done, while the details of these solutions are worked out and implemented.

In my experience, there have been several times when potential conflicts turned into friendships or at least into collegial relationships because of the "win-win" solutions that unexpectedly were created. One attorney, who represented a public agency where I previously worked, came to me with a request for information about a recommendation my staff had made in another agency about a job candidate who now worked for his client. This individual had killed someone on the job and a lawsuit was pending. My report had recommended that the officer not be hired, while this attorney's client had hired the person without conducting an adequate psychological evaluation or checking for previous negative psychological reports.

The lawyer expected me to hand him my report and, at best, give him a brief interpretation of the test results. Instead, I provided him with valuable political and professional information about internal procedures in both agencies that he would have had little chance of discovering without my assistance. Because of this information, he was able to do a much better job advising his client. In return, he assisted me in educating city officials about the ethical and professional issues involved in evaluating officers. Years later, he recommended me for a consulting contract with another organization and I gave him some advice about how to handle a problem he was having with his son. Creating a "win-win" relationship out of a potentially adversarial one was beneficial to both of us.

Recently, a similar situation arose involving a different lawsuit. Without warning, I received a subpoena requiring me to submit hundreds of testing and research documents within a few days to lawyers representing a city agency with which I had no prior contact. The attorneys bringing the lawsuit had listed one of my tests as a possible alternative to what this city previously had used to screen police officers. Due to a change in the law, my listed test was no longer suitable for use in the way they intended and I did not want to hire an attorney to fight for an order of protection. I had to do that once before when a psychologist who did not follow recommended standard procedures, and had misused this same test, issued me a subpoena to help him defend himself in a well-deserved lawsuit. That time, it had cost me several thousand dollars in attorney's fees.

In this case, I saw no reason why I should be required to gather so many documents when they couldn't be used anyway. However, without an order of protection, the law required it. Instead of entering into the adversarial process by hiring an attorney, I successfully negotiated a "win-win" solution with the attorneys who had sent me the subpoena. It was arranged that they would not pursue the subpoena and, in return, I would provide them with information about testing that would help them in their case.

Once you make a conscious effort to search for "win-win" solutions in any potentially adversarial situation, new and creative possibilities will appear more readily. For example, my husband and I own two barns on an old farm property where we take summer vacations. The man who used to own the farm has retained lifetime use of one of the barns. This three-horse barn was built in 1845 with post-and-beam roof construction and still has the original logs with their bark intact in the ceiling of the hayloft. With the man's approval, we fixed the crumbling foundation so that this barn would not fall down and, in the process, changed some of the doors back to their original and smaller sizes. After we had made this barn functional again, and had cleaned out truckloads of garbage and old paint cans so that it was possible to do the restoration work, the local historical society presented us with one of its annual awards for historical preservation.

The next year, the man who uses this barn purchased a large boat and failed to measure its width correctly. It turned out to be a few inches too wide to fit through the new, but old style, doors. One day, he came to me insisting that if I didn't get a carpenter to completely rebuild the wall and doors to the width he needed to store his new boat, he would "put a match to the whole place."

For several weeks we argued back and forth about this situation. I told him that he wouldn't have been able to put anything in the barn, and certainly not a large motorboat, if I hadn't restored the foundation and cleaned out the main floor for him. He argued that it should have been preserved just the way it was when he sold it, two owners before us. At that time, this barn had a metal garage door with paint cans and old tractor motor parts piled to the ceiling in front of it, preventing any vehicle's access. Nothing in the deed specified anything about these issues, as it simply granted him the use of this barn.

Tired of arguing and unwilling to rebuild the newly restored doors, I finally came up with a more creative solution to our problem that worked. I offered to clean out a section of our other barn so that he could use that one for the storage he needed and still maintain his exclusive control over the first barn. I gave him a separate key to the door so that no one would have access except him. After a year had passed, he was so pleased with this unexpected solution, that he gave me the key to the barn he had use of so that I could use it in the summertime. We had both compromised in order to have a "win-win" result rather than a potential lawsuit over such a petty issue.

Whether about barns or business, the best solutions are those that help everyone to get what they need. Figuring out how to go about doing that, with the least amount of hassle and expense, is the challenge.

To implement the **"N"** for **"Negotiate for 'Win-Win' Solutions"**:

1. When you are presented with a problem that appears to require that either you or the other side must lose, think of three ways in which you could compromise and still retain what you absolutely need.

2. When negotiating for something you need, put yourself in the shoes of all of the members of the opposing party and determine what it is that is most important to them.

3. Look outside of the immediate problem area to see if there are compromises or creative solutions that you have not considered due to your own false pride or tunnel vision. Consult with others for a more objective view of the situation.

4. Ask the opposition for suggestions and then modify any proposals with a counteroffer so that you can retain what you need in an eventual compromise.

O - ONE STEP AT A TIME

"The Journey of a Thousand Miles Begins with One Step"

... Lao tsu

I've been putting off the writing of this book for two years now. When I first got the idea, I was too busy to settle down and start the "hard part" of actually doing it. Instead, I procrastinated and did other things. One day, I realized that if I did not start and finish writing about my ideas immediately, I might not have an opportunity to write this book for another two or three years.

How do you start a project as large as writing a book without becoming overwhelmed by the enormity of the task? I finally found my inspiration: ONE STEP AT A TIME! I decided to copy, or temporarily *borrow*, what someone else had done. First, I looked for a book I recently had read on a topic similar to the one I would write. I looked at the number of pages in that book and actually counted up the words on one page. I like the size and type style of the book, so all I needed to do was figure out how much I needed to write each day in order to finish my own book on schedule. It was both easy and doable when I approached the daunting task of book writing this way. I figured out that if I wrote 1500 words, or only two full typewritten pages with a size ten font, each day, I could reach my goal. I decided that it didn't matter *what* I wrote as long as I put my ideas down in a way that I could edit later. This took the pressure off about making it perfect the first time.

There are many ways to keep a task or project under control. Just like studying for a test, it usually is better to do a little bit each day rather than cramming at the last minute. Of course, there are lots of excuses for why we just can't get to it today: There is an audit coming up next week, the company president needs a report yesterday, a meeting, a phone call, the delivery of a refrigerator... you know the routine. Then you forget all of the details explaining why you couldn't do something you wanted to do and sit helplessly at the end of the year asking, "Now why didn't I work on that? It could have been done by now if I just had concentrated more." Unfortunately for all of us, the discipline required to focus on our most important work for years at a time is a learned skill that needs constant practice. Of course, if you *do* manage to work on the most important projects, you then have to accept the fact that there may not be enough time in each day for everything *else* you want to do.

I once was in the audience when an "expert" on organization suggested making a list each day with the three most important things you wish to accomplish. I have found that such a list usually contains two things too many. What has worked for me in recent years is doing *one* thing on that "most important" list each day. I also find it easier to do that one thing early in the day rather than starting other tasks that may distract my attention.

People often ask me how I can accomplish so many things at once: raising a family, running a business, practicing my music, etc... For me, it is all about keeping the focus on the present moment and trying to give full attention to that task or project at hand. It is easy to become distracted. However, if I give myself even ten or fifteen minutes in the beginning of each day to focus on the smallest step towards reaching my long-term goal, such as typing those 1500 words RIGHT NOW, I can do it.

Once that one, most important step for the day has been accomplished, it is time for a rest. I know that anyone reading this who knows me will be laughing right now, but I am serious. Even if it is simply a mental note to yourself that you have done all you really wanted to do today already, you can relax and let the rest of the day unfold. You have met your one-step-is-all-that's-required goal, preferably early in the day, and any additional accomplishments are extra.

I first indulged in the idea of a "that's-enough-personal-accomplishment" party when I finished the requirements for earning my Ph.D. in psychology. I'll never forget the feeling I had walking up a city street one beautiful spring morning to hand in the final copy of my doctoral dissertation to the university library. To explain, I'll digress a little.

I was twenty-four years old at the time and had struggled with a professor for two years who did not appreciate my interests in things other than psychology. I later found out that one of my friends in the same program had told this professor that I was performing in plays while receiving the full fellowship granted to me from the National Institute of Mental Health.

The professor thought that my evenings spent acting were an inappropriate use of my time and, somehow, insulting to her. She also was angry with me for making a joke about planning to get my Ph.D. and then marrying my medical school student boyfriend and having children. The professor had thought that I was serious about giving up psychology and, for two years, I did not understand why she was trying to force me out of her doctoral program. Despite the fact that I had directly asked her for an explanation, I only discovered why she had been so enraged with me several years later when I hired a graduate of that same program to work for me in my psychological testing business. That student had heard the details that finally explained why I had had such a tortured time as a graduate student.

In any case, when I carried the final draft of my dissertation to the library, I said to myself, "You have just accomplished the near impossible. You have worked really hard to do this and have shed a few tears in the process. You really have earned the title 'Doctor' and now you have the choice to keep on working in this field or to retire and do other things with your life. Whatever you do next, no one, not even that professor, can take this accomplishment away."

From that point on, I made a habit of congratulating myself on achieving even the smallest of steps towards larger goals.

Nearly twenty years later, when I decided that it would be fun to learn to sing despite the fact that I was unable to sing on pitch, sounded terrible when I tried, and had been told "not to bother trying," I used this method to keep myself focused and positive.

Perhaps learning to sing for a non-singing person can be seen as the ultimate test for using the principle of "one step at a time." First, most people do not realize that singing is a skill, just like reading English or learning Chinese. While some people are "naturals," most decent singers work at honing specific skills so that they will sound better over time. Since it is not common knowledge that it takes about ten years of training for someone with relative pitch, a sense of which notes are higher or lower than the others, to learn to sing well, quick judgments often are made about those who dare to sing in public. It is interesting that even one missed note, or pitch, will be enough for some people to judge the singer as "no good" or to judge an accomplished singer as "all washed up."

For me, a non-singer trying to sing for the first time, it was important to take off the pressure of singing well. Singing well by audience standards was not in the picture at all in the beginning. Instead, my goal was to sing with fewer and fewer missed notes as time went on. It also was to use the proper techniques to converse with the audience, not to "sing at them." My ultimate goal was to entertain, not necessarily to ever sound like Barbara Streisand or Celine Dion.

Setting achievable goals and then working towards them one step at a time is the real key to getting everything that you want in business and private life. For example, the goals of building sales and building staff are typical in business. However, the daily approach to providing customer service and rapport, that builds sales, and finding talent and encouraging it, that builds a staff, is most important. Both audience appreciation for a singer and sales for a business will materialize when the basics have been covered using a step-by-step approach to fewer flat notes each time out.

To implement the **"O" for "One Step At a Time"**:

1. List five or six tasks or projects you wish to accomplish at the beginning of each day.

2. Pick the most important *single* item on that list and make time to do it.

3. Reward yourself when you have completed that most important task before you go on to the next item on your list. Remind yourself that anything else you manage to accomplish on your list is "icing" because you already have accomplished the primary task for the day.

P – PREPARE TO START OVER WITH PERMISSION TO FAIL

"Success is going from one failure to another with great enthusiasm"

... Winston Churchill

Those who "have it all" often are those who have learned how to start over again and again. Being willing to start from scratch gives people a freedom to develop new businesses, products, or skills that they otherwise might not dare to attempt.

One very successful businessman told me his story of working his way up the corporate ladder after starting out as a newspaper delivery boy. First, he built a small business and then felt helpless as he watched it fail miserably. He was able to pick himself up, though, and by working hard at a new job, soon proved that he still could support himself. After this experience, he knew that he could accomplish anything he wanted to do in the future if he just put his mind to it. This flexibility, along with a survivor's mentality, is very helpful in business. It may be that the experience of failing and then succeeding again helps people to develop the greatest mental strength.

When I started writing music for my children's book, I already was familiar with the sounds of a piano, woodwind instruments, and most stringed instruments found in an orchestra. I had played piano and flute as a child and my older daughter and I had practiced Suzuki violin together for three years. I purchased a sequencing program for my computer that hooked to a keyboard and allowed me to create my own music. When I had learned how to use the program and finished creating the music for seventeen children's songs, I was very pleased with myself. However, a musician who was involved full-time in the music industry listened to my music and remarked that the drum parts I had created on my synthesizer were terrible. In fact, he used more graphic language than that to describe his strong distaste for what I had done.

While I was disappointed with his frank assessment, I couldn't disagree with him. After all, I had never played any drums except for a few toys when I was a child and I had a limited sense of rhythm anyway. I used to sit in the high school band and pick up my flute whenever the girl next to me picked up hers. I really didn't try to do any counting on my own. When this girl was absent one day, I had to take on the position of first flute and lead the section. I had faked it so well for so long that the band teacher was shocked to see how poorly I performed without someone else taking the lead.

Anyway, I decided that the only thing I could do to fix my poor sense of rhythm and my obvious drumming disability was to take a few drum lessons and see what I could learn. I called the local music store and got the name of a drum teacher who lived nearby. I then called this teacher and mentioned that my son and I would like to come for a few lessons together. At the last minute, my son decided not to take the lessons, so I went alone. I felt a little silly asking for drum lessons at my age. My teacher was still in his twenties and it seemed pretty crazy for someone like me suddenly to want to play drums. Most of his students were in the eight to ten age bracket. I was breaking records here!

In any case, I took the first two lessons and I was hooked. It really was fun learning how to hit those drums and I could tell that I would be able to learn how to play quite well if I listened to the teacher. Over the next three years, I took the equivalent of one full year of drum lessons. I practiced and learned enough to know which music tracks sounded like a real drummer was playing and which did not. At the very least, I had a new appreciation for the amount of time and energy drummers must spend on their craft to become proficient.

I reached a new level in starting over after I had been playing drums for about two years. One day, at a lesson, my teacher asked if I would do him a favor. He was playing in an orchestra concert that next Saturday afternoon and then had to go to a gig in a city bar immediately after the concert. Since he was going to be rushing just to make the performance times, he had no time to set up his drums at the bar. He wondered if I would meet a friend of his at the bar who would drop the drum set off. Since he just had taught me how to set up my drum set, he wanted me to practice by setting up his set at a real gig. When I found myself on all fours trying to fix a broken foot pedal on a small, dark and dirty stage in a bar full of people younger than me who were drinking beer and having fun, I knew that if I could do that, I could do anything. Somehow, I actually managed to set up the drums well enough so that when my teacher arrived in the middle of the second song, he was able to start playing immediately. I was so proud. Of course, I also realized that if my friends saw what I was doing with my spare time, they would think that I had lost my mind!

Since then, I have discovered several other large gaps in my music education. To reach my goal of becoming a better musician, I sit in on my daughters' Saturday morning music classes as we play alto saxophones and percussion instruments in jazz and percussion ensembles as part of a conservatory program for high school students. Since I was unable to successfully impersonate a high school student, I have convinced the director and several teachers in this school to let me participate in these classes as the only adult groupie. I truly enjoy the opportunity of spending time with my daughters and with the talented young musicians in the school. I also enjoy the extra bonus of being able to embarrass my teenagers with occasional squeaky notes or with my latest high fashion choice of wearing socks with sandals.

Starting over is a skill that becomes more refined each time you do it. When you first start out, everything is very serious. Young people often feel that they need to show the world that they are grown up and ready to handle jobs and social relationships. When you are older, starting over is more of a risk if your livelihood depends upon new successes. Middle-aged executives who have lost their jobs due to "down-sizing" and the merging of corporations have a particularly difficult time finding new jobs and starting over in new careers. It is only the most resilient among them who can keep a positive attitude and find a new place to work.

On the plus side, there is a certain relief that comes from being at square one again. Being a beginner means that you can ask questions instead of always answering them. It means that you can grow in new directions and challenge yourself in new areas. It means that there are fewer people trying to compete for your current position at the bottom. It also is easier to cope with the problems of starting over when you can remember a history of successes. As my businessman friend learned, once he failed and picked himself up, he never felt helpless again.

Having to start over can turn into an advantage, or a blessing in disguise, as it was for another friend of mine who lost his job and spent a year looking for a new one. Although he had to accept a decrease in pay, he found his new position to be the job that he always wanted. It is a fact that, today, our society requires workers to be more flexible. It now is becoming commonplace for people to have worked in three or more careers and to have started over at least two or more times before they retire. Being prepared to start over by using the knowledge gained from previous experience is essential for people who want to stay in control of their lives and stay on the path that leads to "having it all."

In addition to being prepared to start over, it is important to give yourself and others permission to fail. Whether you are directing employees in a business organization or raising a ten-year old, it is important to create an environment where those you supervise can reach their greatest potential. The only way I know to do this efficiently is to create an atmosphere where people know that if they make a mistake, it is not the end of the world. It is often annoying, frustrating, and sometimes quite costly, when mistakes are made. However, what seems most essential to future growth is that people understand that they will have other opportunities to try again. Without this mindset, it is easy to become discouraged and to decide not to try at all. The "burn-out" often seen in troubled employees may be related to this problem.

This is true in personal life as well. Although many of my friends learned to cook by helping their mothers in the kitchen, mine rarely required her children to help out in this area. Perhaps her view that she could do the job much faster with a lot less mess overrode her interest in having us learn how to cook. In any case, one day, without her permission, my girlfriend and I decided to try our skills at baking a cake. We were probably about nine or ten years old at the time. We had heard that cake ingredients included flour, sugar, milk and eggs, so we mixed some of these together into a pasty concoction. Then we put our mixture into a pan and turned on the oven. The result was a hard, flat, and tasteless kind of pancake. Soon my friend was standing on a chair to put the flour away, when it fell and flour spilled all over the counter and floor.

It was at this time when my mother arrived home from shopping and walked in the door to discover the mess we had made. We tore out of the house and ran next door to hide in my friend's bedroom closet. We figured my mother would never think to look for us there. After my mother marched directly into the neighbor's house and dragged me back home to be punished, I overheard her telling other people this story using the same line to describe the scene: "..And *there* was Janet, standing on my *good* kitchen chair, dropping *all* of the flour all over the floor!"

While Janet and I later laughed about this incident, it is no surprise that I have developed very little interest in cooking as an adult. My mother's desire for tidy techniques in her domain of the kitchen created an environment where I was not permitted to fail. Therefore, I never felt interested or comfortable learning to do anything well in that environment either.

Of course, there were many times when my mother provided the support needed for me to learn how to accept failure gracefully and to understand how I could do something better the next time. When one of my first boyfriends decided that he wanted to date someone else, I didn't understand what had happened or what I had done wrong. Later, I found out that another girl had told this boy some false stories about what I thought about him so that he would go out with her instead. It turned out that the main thing I did wrong was that I did not ask my boyfriend what was going on. I was too proud to confront him and simply accepted other people's observations that he now was with someone else.

In my disappointment over this situation, my mother consoled me, talking about how there were "other fish in the sea," and how I would have another opportunity to communicate better with a boyfriend in the future. Of course, I soon discovered that she was right and eventually learned how I wanted to behave in relationships as new ones developed. In that case, I learned that it was important to speak up about possible miscommunications before others fill in the gaps for you.

Behaving in a socially appropriate manner is a learned set of responses based largely upon trial and error. No matter how many books are read on a subject of interest, it is the experience of accepting failures gracefully while experimenting in that area that results in the greatest learning over time. Having important people around you willing to accept your failures, as well as your successes, adds the support needed to try again.

I have seen this same situation occur in the workplace. Insecure managers, who are afraid that others may catch them making a mistake, or employees, who are afraid that someone else may come in and take over their jobs, often behave in an overprotective and uncooperative manner. They do this out of a fear of their own failure or fear of being discovered as a fraud. Often, these people are quite talented, yet they are so afraid of making errors that they shut out others and limit their own opportunities in the process.

One of my friends is the manager of several hundred employees in a large business that involves gambling. She is an honest person who has been promoted several times because of her attention to details and ability to get along with the people she supervises. Recently, she was promoted to a new job that involves supervising several managers of different areas. The last time I talked with her, she complained about how one of the new managers she is supervising is making it impossible for her to do her job. She has tried several ways to find out exactly what this manager is doing on her job, but the manager leaves notes when she is away that no one is to touch anything on her computer. When asked for information about what she is doing, this manager answers my friend with curt responses that reveal minimal information. Since this manager handles some of the organization's money, my friend wonders if her employee is doing something corrupt or if the woman is simply afraid that if someone else understands the details of how she does her job, she could be replaced.

In my company, there also have been past employees who developed niches in the business where they were the only ones who really knew how to do certain procedures. Since their occasional absence from work created instant problems and, once, a near crisis, we have worked to cross-train both managers and general employees to avoid this situation in the future. While some people may be more insecure about their positions, and more protective about what they do, it is important to create an atmosphere where some failures are acceptable as long as they don't reoccur exactly the same way again.

The antidote to failure is the promotion of a strong belief in yourself and in the fact that your efforts eventually *will* pay off.

132

It is encouraging to watch athletes return to Olympic competition after experiencing embarrassing defeats in front of the world four years earlier. When there is determination to win, and competitors focus on the details of the job at hand, they can triumph.

One television announcer, who had been an athlete herself, recently commented that a faltering Olympian had the physical talent to win at world-class competition, but not the inner confidence. As he was performing, she remarked, "This guy just doesn't believe, deep down, that he can consistently complete this skill. That is what hurts him in competition." The very next day, this same athlete found the courage to press on regardless of what people were saying about him. In his final events, he demonstrated that he could perform under pressure and went home with the high scores that proved it. By acknowledging initial failure, accepting it, and determining to change the course of future events, it is possible to get what you want in life.

To implement the **"P"** for **"Prepare to Start Over with Permission to Fail"**:

1. Find something you never have done before and take the first steps needed to develop that activity or skill. Don't stop practicing until you have made at least five mistakes.

2. Give yourself a list of too much work to do in one day. Then try to do it all anyway, giving yourself permission to fail if you haven't completed everything in that one day. The point is to try to do the impossible with permission to fail.

3. List three times when you failed at something that was too hard for you at the time. Think of how you reacted (i.e. what you said to yourself about your abilities and self-worth). Then write how you plan to react to similar situations in the future.

Q – QUIT COMPLAINING & MAKING EXCUSES

"Why Put Off Till Tomorrow What You Can Do Today?"

What *is* it about complaining that is so attractive for so many of us? How much of each day is spent building up work for a complaint department or listening to others do the same? How much gossiping about what others have done wrong is going on in your office on a daily basis?

Apparently, the details of the situation really don't matter. Wherever people gather, there will be an expression of disappointment over something that isn't right. Without much effort, you probably can name a relative or friend who rarely does anything but complain and then name another one who is full of excuses. While we all may have some natural inclination to complain at times, it is the habit and constant practice of this activity that can slow our progress.

I recently heard about an organization that provides virtually unlimited funding for its employees to conduct the research projects of their choice. It is an ideal setting where the researchers, who each have top credentials in their field of science, can maximize their potential, experiment in new areas, travel as much as they desire, earn good salaries and pensions for the future, and be quite secure and protected for years in their careers. Regardless of the fact that these researchers are in a most unusual work setting, and most of them will admit this readily, they still spend a great deal of time complaining about their work and about the administration of the organization.

The fear of starting a new project or venture often keeps even the best-intentioned individuals far from the action. Making excuses for why things cannot possibly be accomplished is an art that usually has been perfected by those who cannot bring themselves to take the necessary steps towards reaching their goals.

As a psychotherapist, I worked with several groups of social phobics who were determined to conquer their fears. Pam, a woman who suffered panic attacks at the thought of going out with other people, was given an assignment to complete before the next week's session. Her "homework" was to go over to her church's BINGO game. She was not asked to go inside or even to pay at the door. The idea was that she would, at first, just go through the motions of getting herself physically *near* to a social event.

When this woman returned to the group the following week, she admitted that she had not made it out of her house to the BINGO game. Despite the fact that she had agreed earlier that the task was doable and that she was willing to go to the church, Pam had come up with a good excuse. She carefully explained to the group that she had to do her laundry that Wednesday and when she went to get dressed for BINGO, her "underwear was still drying". Of course, she couldn't *possibly* go to the church with wet underwear, so she cancelled her plans. After other group members discussed some options she might have had, such as finding some old underwear to wear for that evening, Pam admitted that her wet underwear story might be a bit weak. Months later, group members referred back to the problem of having "wet underwear" whenever someone made excuses about why they had to avoid a situation. By realizing how ridiculous excuses can be, many of my clients were able to rise above their past habits and conquer their fears.

There are times when people who work or live together create a negative atmosphere that is very difficult to change. A typical hint of inaction is when a great deal of time is spent complaining and gossiping about what is wrong with others. When I first started working for one organization, I took my meal breaks in the staff lunchroom. The same group was there everyday. After a few months, I became aware of feeling low rather than re-energized after these breaks. I realized that it had to do with the nature of the conversations I was hearing in that lunchroom. After these staff members finished a stream of complaints about

135

work, mostly petty complaining about bosses, co-workers or workloads, their conversation turned to what else was wrong in their lives, how awful someone looked in the newspaper, or how much trouble they were having with their spouses or children. Very little time was spent talking about positive subjects and I later decided to take my breaks at a different time with people who did less complaining and criticizing in general.

Of course, just today I have been complaining about how my computer keeps doing the wrong thing and how the coffee I just made for my houseguest tastes terrible. It is most likely my problem on both counts. It seems that complaining and making excuses may provide an immediate outlet so that we can feel better about ourselves. It also is true that, despite our many shortcomings, we may feel more comfortable with ourselves believing that most of the problem is out *there*. Even though our comfort level may *seem* to be enhanced by having others listen to our complaints and agree that our problems are, indeed, caused by others, we may be doing ourselves a disservice by over-reliance on this defense.

Maintaining a positive self-image in order to continue doing our work and managing our complicated lives is essential. However, if we cut back on the excuses and whining just a bit, we actually may have more time to solve some of the problems we face. For example, there was a boy in my high school class who moaned about his "terrible" ski equipment whenever he fell, which was frequently. He would fly down the mountain completely out of control. Then, after he had crashed head first into a snow bank, everyone on the hill could hear his voice screaming, "These bindings are such ^^**^# garbage!" He would have done a lot better if he had asked his friends what was wrong and gotten some help with his skiing technique, which was the *real* problem.

There is a significant amount of maintenance that comes with "having it all" and that takes away from the time most successful people have left for gossiping or complaining. Being aware of

how these time-wasters can invade your life is the first step
toward keeping them at a distance.

To implement the "Q" for "Quit Complaining & Making
Excuses":

1. For one day, listen carefully to what you say to others
   and count the number of times when you hear yourself
   complaining to someone else.

2. Write each complaint you made and what you are going
   to do to keep from complaining about the same thing in
   the future. This can include simply accepting the
   situation or learning how to make better coffee.

3. Mark which complaints still seem necessary in order for
   you to blow off steam.

4. Notice which people around you are chronic complainers
   and which people tend to apply themselves to their work
   and play activities rather than complaining.

5. Make a point of reducing the time you spend talking
   with someone else who tends to complain frequently. If
   you can't reduce that time, try to compensate by doing
   something that is positive and fun for the same amount
   of time.

R - RECOGNIZE & REWARD COLLEAGUES AND CO-WORKERS

"Catch people doing something good"

Whether you are busy managing a department in a company or building a business for yourself, it is easy to overlook the "small stuff" around you. This can be a real problem if what you overlook are your own employees. Most of the time, managers spend their efforts dealing with the most pressing problems of the day: a dissatisfied customer, a new law that may change the way business can be conducted, a broken phone or computer system, or an employee who isn't doing his job properly. Unfortunately, more damage can be done to a company's future when good employees are ignored for the sake of solving everyday problems.

One year, while building my company, I hired a young woman to work for me. She was very polite at all times and appeared to be very efficient. This was a time when I was doing a lot of traveling to trade conventions and wasn't able to spend much time in the office. I was so busy that I had developed the bad habit of assigning work to people and then forgetting to ask about it for days or even weeks at a time. This particular woman had an office on a different floor than mine and busied herself with numerous tasks I had assigned. After a few months, she resigned from her position, saying that her physician husband wanted her to stay at home, or, at least, not to travel so far to get to work everyday.

I took her words at face value and didn't question her reasons for leaving. Since I always had a most pleasant speaking relationship with her, I assumed that everything had been fine on my end. On her last day, I thanked her for her time, wished her good luck, and she left my office. A few days later, I went downstairs to her office to check her desk before giving it to a new employee. To my surprise and dismay, I found piles of completed work, in perfect order, which I had not seen or even asked about during her time spent working for me. She had been too timid to tell me what she had done, but she had completed the work of three people while she was there. I had shirked my responsibility to this employee by not knowing about, much less rewarding, her quiet and quite exceptional efforts.

The idea that there are hidden gems in every population of potential workers was driven home to me later in a different situation. I was working as a consultant to a large public safety agency. My job was to test thousands of officer candidates each year and to help the department reject those who were most "unsuitable." During this time, I was unhappy with the ability level of some of my own employees. Even though several of them had bachelor's degrees, they seemed to be functioning at a junior high school level or less. I realized that education alone does not assure that people can handle simple academic problems.

My goal was to create a quick test that would let me know if a job candidate could solve problems at a high school or college level. My son's advanced math class was working from a fifth grade book at the time, so I borrowed his book and read the word problems in it. Then I developed a twelve-item word problem test that had questions about standard business issues, such as how much it would cost to order a certain number of materials from a catalog, or how much an employee would earn with a specific number of vacation days and benefits. Since these were the kind of problems an employee might need to solve in the workplace, I thought the test would be appropriate for use in employee screening.

I tested this new instrument out on my friends, neighbors, and employees who were willing to take it and gave them a thirty-minute time limit. In some cases, and to my great surprise, their responses were loud and angry. For one thing, I was reminding them of those "awful" word problems that they had to solve back in school and, for another thing, I was testing them again on how fast they could think through problems, which they resented.

The word problems were simple, or at least fifth grade simple, but I had put in extra information that needed to be ignored in order to calculate the correct answer. This made the problems more difficult even though the actual procedures needed to solve them were at an upper elementary school level.

I soon had figured out the average number of items that people from different professions and educational levels would correctly answer on this test. For good computer programmers, engineers, and professional scientists, ten to twelve of these problems were solvable. For a good administrative assistant, the range was from six to eight correct answers. My son was able to answer four of the items correctly, while my incompetent employee with the bachelor's degree got only two questions right. My professional friends who were in fields such as management, psychology, business, or publishing tended to correctly answer between seven and eight items on this test.

Next, it was time to try the test out on entry-level job candidates. I had the opportunity to test hundreds of correction officer applicants who were mostly young adult males with a high school diploma or the equivalency. This group's average number of correct answers on this test, now called the *Hilson Cognitive Abilities Test (HCAT)*, was three to four.

What amazed me, though, was that in every group of fifty or so candidates, one person would score at least a ten or eleven on the *HCAT.* This was better than the average score for professional managers. When I investigated further, I found that the candidates who attained the highest scores were usually candidates whose background information was otherwise unimpressive.

Scores on this test identified general math problem-solving skills that also reflected problem-solving abilities at work, or the lack thereof, as I had found in some of my own employees. I was surprised that there was little else to note in the records of these high-scoring candidates and thought how easy it might be for them to slip through the cracks as average workers just as they seemed to have done in their lives so far. I then informed the department administrators about which entry-level candidates might have exceptional potential for jobs requiring this type of problem-solving skill. It was my hope that the administration could provide challenging jobs for the most talented candidates once they were identified.

I realized that it is the responsibility of a good manager to find people with special talents, perhaps talents that the people, themselves, do not recognize. In fact, facilitating talent in those around you may be one of the most rewarding parts of successfully running a department or managing a business. As in raising a child who may someday aid you in your old age, the value of talent facilitation in employees extends to a future when your livelihood may depend on the team of workers you have put together in your organization.

Finally, it is not enough to recognize people's talents. An effective manager also needs to learn how to recognize and reward special employee efforts properly. I made a mistake in my business one day when my staff and I finally had finished writing a lengthy technical manual for a new test. This project lasted for over six months. Everyone in the office had made some contribution, though one staff member had done the bulk of the work herself. I wanted to thank everyone for working together so diligently on the project, so I bought a bottle of champagne, some cheese and crackers, and called a meeting.

With the staff sitting around in a circle, I thanked the group. I then proceeded to name each person and mentioned what they had done, whether big or small. When I got to the person who had done most of the work, I thanked her briefly for her contributions to the writing of the manual. I thought I had done a good job of recognizing everyone's work and enjoyed the spontaneous party I had thrown. Around that time, I probably had read in a business book somewhere that you should compliment your employees and regularly notice something good that they have done.

Later, the woman who had completed the majority of the work on the manual came to me in tears. She felt slighted and insulted by my equal inclusion of the other staff members in my comments about the manual. I had not singled her out as the most important contributor and she felt that I had underestimated her major role. In fact, I thought that I should include everyone else so that they would feel they were part of a team. I learned my lesson that day and have since tried to make sure that special employee efforts get the public appreciation they deserve.

While many people have to work because they need the money, they work hard because they want to earn respect and appreciation for utilizing special work-related skills. Once annual raises and employee benefits match those of other employers, it is the way managers help employees to feel appreciated for their hard work that earns their loyalty. If they have not done the work, as in the case of my staff members who had made minor contributions to that manual, good employees will not be upset if another person is singled out and praised. In fact, this demonstrates that if they make a special effort themselves, they, too, will be recognized.

To implement the **"R"** for **"Recognize and Reward Colleagues and Co-Workers"**:

1. Identify three people at work who have done something for you this week that has helped you in your job. Make a point of telling each of these three people how much you appreciate what they have done to make your job easier.

2. Find something you can do for them in return or ask how you can help them in their jobs.

3. Find a different way to express your appreciation for

142

something someone in your life has done for you recently. If you usually do the same thing, such as sending flowers, find a new gift or way to show your gratitude.

S – STAND OUT IN A CROWD

"All Publicity is Good Publicity"

When all is said and done, standing out is usually a very good thing in business. If you can put yourself in the spotlight, even for a moment, people will remember you later even if they don't remember exactly why. Keeping the saying in mind that "all publicity is good publicity" can help you to reach your goals. This is because if you put yourself "out there," ready to be counted and ready to take advantage of opportunities when they present themselves, you will have a better chance of succeeding than if you wait for someone else to ask you to make an appearance.

Sometimes you have to take risks or even feel a little embarrassed in order to stand out. One time, I found myself at an annual convention reception with about two hundred people. I was waiting for an executive manager from a different state to finish talking with some clients so that we could go to dinner and discuss a testing program for his company. As the reception wound down, the other females left the room. Most of them had accompanied their spouses to this party and were not part of the business conversations taking place among the men. As I waited for my potential client, I suddenly realized that I was the only female in the entire room. To amuse myself, I counted sixty-one men, mostly sales managers, in dark business suits and myself. I certainly *was* standing out and several men came over to me to ask me who I was *with* and what I was doing there.

I considered leaving the room because I was beginning to feel uncomfortable. The assumption on the part of a few bored managers was that I was waiting for a "hot date" with my potential client. However, I wanted to meet with this man and knew that if I left and came back, I might miss the opportunity. When we later returned from dinner to continue our conversation in a hospitality suite set up by this manager's company, the "knowing" glances and smirks continued. By this time, I didn't care. I had built a rapport with my new client that would not have been as easy to do over the telephone or through the mail and I had received some valuable advice from him on how to increase sales in my company. I took the opportunity to stand out, literally, and it was worth the effort.

A few years later, when another of the managers who had been in that room was promoted in his job with a different company, he called me to develop a testing program for his employees. Even though I had felt uneasy waiting for my client at that party, my presence ultimately had a very positive effect and my business grew because of the new contacts I was able to make. While I was embarrassed at the time, I now regularly look for opportunities to stand out in a crowd.

Helping others to become aware of your talents and achievements is something that can bring long-term rewards. Conversely, the benefits that can come from achievement will not be realized if those achievements are so closely guarded that few people know about them. An example of this situation occurred a few years ago when my younger daughter started training in rhythmic gymnastics at a local community center. On the day of my daughter's first competition in this sport, the coach told me that she was going to stop coaching the next year. The manager of the community center wanted to cut the hours when the girls could practice and the coach said that she was tired of handling most of the team responsibilities and paperwork herself.

For the past five years, she had been coaching girls from the neighborhood, driving in from her home in another state, sometimes even driving out of her way to pick up the girls who did not have transportation to the center. She had trained this team in a small area of a noisy gymnasium with basketball players on the other side. Frequently, basketballs would land in the middle of the mat where the girls practiced their routines. Also, the parents of most of these girls could not afford to pay high coaching fees and there was little money available to cover the expenses of this team.

Despite the less than optimal conditions, the team had grown and the girls had learned how to compete in this sport. With dedication and talent, this coach had trained her girls so well that they won state and regional championships and even one Junior Olympic medal. When I asked if the city agency that ran the community center knew of these achievements, the answer was "no." Even though one of the girl's medals was listed in the national gymnastics magazine, few people on the local level even knew that this team existed!

I was shocked that such a successful team, sponsored in part by a city organization, was hidden from public view. I convinced this coach to stay for another year and see what would happen if we launched a publicity campaign. It was easy to get articles published in local newspapers since the idea of a community center's team of young girls who were winning medals in an Olympic sport was very attractive.

Within four years, thirty-five news articles were published about this team, including photos of the girls and their coach. A second coach was hired, while the first coach continued on a part-time basis, and the team members went on to win gold medals at national and international competitions. Some individuals who saw the newspaper articles made contributions. Local businesses also contributed money after they were contacted by parents who now could show them what the girls had accomplished. The relationship between the team and the manager of the center improved significantly as it became public knowledge that she and her center were sponsoring a young girl's championship team. When the team hosted a weekend exhibition and performed their routines for the community, new girls were recruited to the training program, the public was entertained, and both the center and the team benefited.

The initial goal of this publicity campaign was to help city administrators become aware of the team's existence so that the community center would be less inclined to reduce practice hours or raise fees beyond what the team could afford. The other goal was to give the girls and their coaches some recognition for what they had achieved. While both goals were met, there have been additional benefits from the effort to help this team stand out in the community.

Recently, a large bookstore invited my daughter and another gymnast to be guest speakers at a children's story telling program during the time of the Olympics. They were asked to read a short children's book about gymnastics and then to talk and answer questions about their own experiences. The community relations manager for this large bookstore had been following the careers of these gymnasts through the numerous published articles and came up with the program's idea based on these articles.

Clearly, the effort of publicizing this team's achievements has led to continuing opportunities for growth and future achievement. The bookstore launched its own publicity campaign that resulted in the attendance of two reporters at the program. This led to additional articles and photos that were published about the girls and their accomplishments. With an invitation to compete in Japan next year, these athletes have a new goal and more people around to help them achieve it.

It is not uncommon for people to avoid publicity or the spotlight for fear of how others will view them. They may worry that they will be seen as arrogant or conceited if they try to stand out in a crowd or fear that a reporter will print something that makes them look silly or stupid. Even though we all like to analyze everything we see and put a name or label on it, it is important to remember that appearances are deceiving. Since people will form a first impression of you *anyway*, and it may or may not be accurate, worrying about how you appear to others is bound to be a waste of time.

One morning, I watched an excellent keynote speaker begin a speech in front of two thousand human resources professionals at a convention breakfast. She spoke for the first few minutes using a speech pattern and accent that may have suggested to her audience that she was a minimally educated woman. When she then dropped the accent and characterization, the audience was shocked and the point was made that appearances are deceiving and "you can't judge a book by its cover."

I once was invited to give a lecture in Nebraska sponsored by the State Attorney General there. Private transportation from this lecture back to Omaha was provided by a state trooper who landed our helicopter in the V.I.P. section of the airport. I was excited to discover, on my arrival, that President Bush's two airplanes and about twenty-five staff members and security personnel were standing near where we had landed. As I stepped out of the helicopter and walked toward the terminal, I was able to see the red carpet inside Air Force One and looked at the people standing around. I wondered who they were and what it must be like to work with a president. Suddenly, I noticed that they were staring back at me with the same interest. Once I was inside the terminal, I realized that *I* was the one who had appeared to be the celebrity! After all, I had just stepped off of a private helicopter and was escorted through the middle of their high security area by a six-foot tall trooper in uniform. Just as I was so impressed by them, they were wondering about the identity of that woman with the briefcase!

It is not always easy to allow yourself to "stand out." From our first days in school, we are taught to conform and to stay in our proper seats. When a child deviates from that norm, he or she often is ostracized from "the group." For example, in junior high school, I was told by a male friend that I would never find a steady boyfriend if I kept doing things like beating the boys in ping-pong. His suggestion that I lose on purpose in order to be seen as more "feminine" confused me at first. However, I finally ignored his well-intentioned suggestion and persevered until I met someone who could appreciate my athletic abilities.

In any case, it often takes a special effort for talented young adults to break their childhood habits of conformity and allow for creativity and special strengths to shine. This is especially true when peer pressure operates to employee's disadvantage in the workplace.

In one agency, where I was working as a consultant, hard workers regularly were told to slow down by their peers so that they wouldn't make the lazier workers "look bad." When the boss was out of the area, paying personal bills while wearing a Walkman's headphones and eating McDonald's breakfasts on company time was standard practice. In this kind of situation, the only effective response for a person who wants to "have it all" is to change the work environment to one where hard work and dedication are rewarded more frequently.

I once watched one outstanding employee refuse to cave in to the negative attitudes directly promoted by his co-workers. He worked hard regardless of his surroundings and the suggestions by co-workers that he was doing too much work everyday. When he finally got a good job offer somewhere else and was planning to leave this organization, I got permission from his boss to offer him a job in my own company. By "standing out," working hard, and daring to be different, he substantially increased his career opportunities and earning potential. Allowing yourself to be in a position to show your skills often helps you to get where you are going faster.

To implement the **"S"** for **"Stand Out in a Crowd"**:

1. Think of a time when you held yourself back at work for fear of standing out too much. Then write down the positive things that might have occurred if you had allowed yourself to be in the spotlight.

2. Watch for opportunities that come your way to stand out or to participate more fully in work-related activities. Write down two ways you can increase your visibility at

work, such as showing your boss a new project idea or asking for expanded responsibilities.

3. Make an effort to do something at work this week that demonstrates one of your strengths to someone who may not be aware of this quality or ability.

T – TIMING CAN MAKE ALL THE DIFFERENCE

"Strike While the Iron is Hot"

Watching for opportunities and then working to make them work for you is one of the keys to success in many areas of life. Good timing, sometimes referred to as good *luck*, is something that cannot be bottled, but it can be taken advantage of repeatedly.

I once met the highly respected Broadway actress, Geraldine Fitzgerald. After enjoying a very successful career in the theatre, she admitted how she had gotten her first "break" in show business. She had arrived early one day for a general casting call at a theatre when a man rushed out of the wings, telling her that the director would see her "right away." Apparently, he thought she was the actress scheduled for a special audition prior to the regular one. Without missing a beat, this actress jumped at the opportunity. She auditioned and, by the time the casting people realized that they had made a mistake, she already had been cast in her first major role.

While it could be said that she was 'lucky' to have been mistaken for someone else, this actress did not rely upon luck for her actual audition. She was well prepared to demonstrate her acting skills and would have been ready at any time when the opportunity eventually presented itself.

I often am asked how I happened to become involved in the law enforcement field. It was a similar story of taking an opportunity and making it work. I thought that I was going to be laid off from my job, so I signed up to receive job notices through the placement office at my old school. When I found out that I still would be able to work at my old job, I discarded the job notices when they arrived. After six months, when I was not looking for employment, I received the final month's notices in the mail. A letter advised me that this would be the last

151

mailing, so I thought that I should look at it before I threw it away.

I saw a notice that seemed to describe my relatively few qualifications at the time quite perfectly. A city agency was looking for someone with expertise in anxiety disorders or stress as well as knowledge of personality tests. In fact, my graduate program had focused on the specific test that was mentioned in the ad and I had been running therapy groups with people who suffered from anxiety and panic attacks for two years.

Since I no longer was looking for a new job, I doubt that I would have gone to the trouble of mailing out a resume. However, I saw a local phone number at the bottom of the ad and, on a whim, dialed it. When I spoke with the person who had placed the ad, she was excited to hear that I worked in a phobia clinic since she once had suffered from a phobia herself. She invited me to come to her office for an interview and assured me that the job was a consulting position that would not take up very much of my time.

As I have mentioned, one of my big problems is that I usually get lost whenever I have to go somewhere new and I also am one of the world's worst direction followers. Not too surprisingly, I did manage to get lost, once again, trying to find this woman's office. Although I had left early, with plenty of time to do my usual "wandering-around-trying-to-find-the-place" routine, I managed to get myself on the wrong express subway in New York City. It passed my destination without stopping and then continued into another *county* before I could get off. I had not realized that subways even *did that,* though I had been living in this city for several years.

I wasn't sure what I should do since now I would be at least forty-five minutes late for the appointment. Despite problems with directions, I never had been late for any business appointment before. The consulting job was with a public safety agency and I knew that arriving that late was unlikely to make a very good impression. However, the idea of not arriving at all seemed worse, so I decided to go to the woman's office anyway.

When I finally did arrive, nearly one hour late, I sat down in a chair in the reception area to wait for the receptionist who was not at her desk. Within no longer than thirty seconds from the time I had taken a seat, the woman I was supposed to meet came huffing and puffing into the room. She began to apologize profusely, saying that she was so sorry to have kept me waiting and hoped that I hadn't been too inconvenienced by her delay. I graciously told her that it was *perfectly* all right. She ushered me into her office and we proceeded to talk about the consulting position, which she offered me within an hour.

It turned out that this job was a wonderful opportunity for me to use the skills I had learned in school and in my previously limited professional work experience. I took the position, never dreaming that this consulting job would soon turn into a full-time career or that I would have the opportunity to help develop the new field of police psychology based on my experiences in this organization. As with Geraldine Fitzgerald, I was lucky to be allowed to "try out" for the job at all, but it was my determination and preparation to do the future work that took me the rest of the way. The idea here is to enjoy the circumstances of good timing and good luck by being prepared to take advantage of unexpected opportunities.

To implement the **"T"** for **"Timing Can Make All the Difference**:

1. Arrive thirty minutes early for at least one event or appointment this week. Write down what additional information you discovered or who you met due to your early arrival.

2. When the timing is right or you have luck on your side, take advantage of opportunities by being prepared. Think of a new skill you would like to be prepared with

at all times. Practice that skill daily so that you always will be ready for the situation when timing, along with preparation, can make all the difference.

U – "USE FEAR TO MOTIVATE ACTION"

**"Push the infinite as far as you can.
You can always push it farther. Do not fear"**

... Helen Keller

One of my friends told me this story about her Hungarian stepfather, Philip. As an immigrant to the United States at the beginning of World War II, he came to this country without any money, knowing only a few words of English. He obtained his first job as a salesman with an insurance company. On his first day at work, his boss told him that he would be required to make at least one outside sales call each day. Since he didn't understand English very well, Philip misunderstood his employer and thought that he meant that salesmen were expected to make at least one *sale* each day.

Since he believed that this was the only way he could keep his job, Philip never called his boss or returned to his office until he had closed the required sale for the day. Of course, this made him an exceptional producer in the company and he soon became known in the insurance industry as "One-a-Day Philip." Because of his outstanding debut in this field, his reputation grew and he earned high commissions. Compared to other salespeople in his company, he also made many more contacts and friends. With time, Philip was promoted within his organization and eventually was able to buy his own insurance business. He died at the age of seventy-five, a multimillionaire and president of a large insurance company. Initially motivated by a misunderstanding and the fear of losing his position, his actions led to exceptional job performance and long-term success.

Instead of allowing fear to immobilize you, it can be used to your advantage. Even the most seasoned entertainers often comment that they never lose their nervousness just before a performance. It may be that anxiety that propels people into

155

making a better effort than they would make if they were completely relaxed.

Philip's wife, Lisa, also became successful as a result of allowing fear to motivate positive career choices. At the age of sixteen, long before she met Philip, she became pregnant and was told by her family that she would have to work to help pay for the rent. Rather than take a menial office or service job, Lisa decided that, since she had to work at something anyway, it was time to find an exciting career. After having her baby, she commuted into Manhattan and began a tireless hunt for modeling jobs. She took any job in that area and soon was able to work as a fitting model. Because she had to take care of her child, she often brought her baby with her on jobs and soon had talked her way into obtaining work as a mother-daughter team. With her outgoing personality, this work led to modeling jobs in print advertising and to a steady career.

Still interested in furthering her goal of having an exciting and lucrative career, Lisa made a second change in direction. One day, she decided to move to California where acting roles were becoming available on television shows. Members of her family ridiculed her and warned that she was bound to fail in Hollywood. Even though she had managed to become secure in her New York modeling career, she was fearful that it would not last. Her child was growing up and she, herself, would not be able to work as a model for many more years.

Motivated by the fear of not being able to support herself and her family for the long-term, Lisa sold what she owned and headed west. Within a short period of time, Lisa's daughter was working as an actress in television. She began with small supporting parts and her mother helped her to work her way up in this competitive business. In her teens, Lisa's daughter obtained a prestigious role in one of the most popular weekly television shows at that time. She worked steadily in acting jobs throughout her childhood, including a featured role on Broadway and a leading movie role.

Although Lisa's daughter became a writer as an adult, her childhood career as an actress supported her family very well. The family members who had made fun of Lisa for her efforts later accepted tickets to performances and bragged about their relative who worked with the big stars in Hollywood. Growing up with the other child stars in Hollywood, Lisa's daughter had interesting experiences and developed friendships that later became the focus of one of her novels. Had it not been for difficult times and the fear that she would not be able to pay the rent if she didn't work very hard, Lisa might not have developed the courage to strike out on her own and follow her dreams. She used her problems and fears to fuel new activities that led to success.

There were a few times in business when I, too, was motivated by fear to do something new. The first time was when I started a consulting job where I was expected to interview candidates for public safety positions. The candidates had been given a psychological test that was supposed to tell whether they had significant emotional problems or evidence of psychopathology. When I began the interviews, I started by interviewing anyone who showed high scores on the scales of this test. After a few interviews, it dawned on me that I didn't have any idea how candidates *without* the elevated scores would respond to interview questions. I thought that it would be a good idea to interview everyone who took the test, at least for a while, so that I would have a better idea about the entire candidate population.

When I was given permission from my employer to interview all of the candidates, I made an interesting discovery. I found that some of the candidates who had apparently normal profiles on their tests admitted to undocumented criminal behavior and to other problems that made them unsuitable for the job. Since they were going to be authorized to carry a gun, my job was to make sure that they did not have any psychological or behavioral problems that would make carrying a weapon dangerous to the community.

One candidate yawned at the end of his interview as he was walking out the door. I asked him if he was tired and he answered that he was exhausted because he hadn't slept much the night before. I asked him why that was, and he answered, "Well, my old lady got in my face and I had to slap her around awhile." On further questioning, he admitted to physically abusing his girlfriend on more than one occasion. I asked another candidate if he had ever done anything against the law when he had not been caught. He answered that, one time, he had helped his friend load a truck full of stolen shoes that were "just sitting there behind the shoe factory." When I asked why he had done that, he answered, "Well, in that situation, I *couldn't* tell my friend that I wouldn't *help* him. He was my friend, after all." Another candidate admitted that she had been in trouble for prostitution even though that information had not been revealed on either the background investigation or the current psychological testing procedure.

When candidates told me about previously unrevealed information that would disqualify them from becoming a public safety officer, I started to worry about my role in the agency's selection process. I had received my license to practice psychology only a year before starting this job and had no experience in the law enforcement field. Since I had so little experience, I was afraid that the information I reported from these interviews might be challenged. I was aware of the lawsuits regarding inappropriate selection procedures and worried that a rejected candidate might sue the department and me for making arbitrary decisions without the appropriate information to support them.

These job applicants were telling me about their misdeeds because, it seemed, they thought that some of these things were impressive. However, if they thought they had been denied a job because of it, they might deny ever telling me about their activities. Basically, I worried, "Why should a judge believe me?!" I also had learned in graduate school that validation studies of tests were required, especially if they were used to deny someone a job. The test that was being used in this agency did not have any studies about its accuracy in predicting the performance of public safety officers.

In the field of psychology, there are specific guidelines for the use of testing and selection instruments and procedures. I had studied these guidelines and believed that there were several areas where disgruntled applicants might successfully challenge this agency's procedures even though it was nearly impossible to meet every guideline. It was directly as a result of my fear of being challenged for basing so much of my decision on an unverified interview, and test that did not have appropriate research, that I began to conduct validation studies on my procedures.

I also attended psychology and police conferences so that I could find out what other people were doing in this same situation. When I discovered that no one in psychology had developed any predictive measures for law enforcement officer evaluations, I realized that there was nothing I could find or purchase from the outside that would help me to do a better job for this agency.

Although I later discovered that this was an opportunity to make a significant contribution, my initial plan was to find out what everyone else was doing and to do the same thing. Instead, from the extra work I undertook, I eventually developed and validated my own test that had many of the same questions I found so effective in the interviews. Years later, after I had developed a thriving test publishing business, some psychologists would make remarks suggesting that I had planned this or that I was a clever businesswoman who had plotted to take over the industry. I used to be offended by these comments, hurt that my zealous interest in doing the right thing in the field of psychology was reduced to a calculated effort to make money. Now I just take such comments as a compliment and laugh, remembering how my initial motivation was simply the fear of being sued!

The second time I was motivated by fear to do something different was when I first began giving lectures about psychology. At that time, I relied on notes and sometimes read from my research papers in order to make sure that the information I was reporting was correct. This made for exceptionally boring presentations that nearly put me to sleep as well as my audience. Despite my poor techniques at the podium, I was invited to give a twenty-minute talk at a prestigious international conference to be held at the FBI Training Academy on a Marine Corps base near Washington, D.C. I was flattered and petrified. I knew that this lecture would be given in front of over one hundred selected conference attendees who were well-known experts in their fields and knew something about my subject as well. I also knew that I had a terrific potential to blow the opportunity by being so boring that no one would want to listen to what I had to say.

Through fear, I became motivated to do something about my poor lecture techniques, which represented a major professional weakness. I attended a conference prior to the one where I was to give my lecture. Instead of meeting with clients, I spent more time than usual attending other speaker's presentations. I watched how they talked with their audiences and imagined myself in their shoes, saying the same things. I watched how the audiences responded and became fascinated with the smallest details of the speakers' actions, including when they walked to the side of the room or when they paused for a drink or for a question. I watched how they managed to stay on track and finish their talks at the appropriate time. My own lectures often ended somewhere in the middle of the material I had hoped to present. Then I would rush around trying to distribute handouts to audience member before they left the room.

In my effort to be better organized for my next lecture, I carefully wrote my new lecture notes and organized the three main points that I wanted to make. I decided that if I was able to explain these ideas clearly to the audience, I would be satisfied. I also listened to the opening remarks made by different lecturers. The most immediately effective speakers were the ones who began their presentations with a few jokes to relax themselves and the audience.

Unfortunately, I knew that telling jokes was at the very end of the list of activities that I could do. Usually, I forgot both the joke and its punch line, even if I thought it was funny when I first heard it. I remembered the time when I had tried to tell a joke at a lecture in front of two hundred people. I had mixed up the punch line, reversing the characters and leaving everyone staring at me in anticipation of hearing something at least mildly amusing. Instead, without immediately realizing what I had done, I stood there looking bewildered that they hadn't laughed at my joke. I decided that I would try to tell a joke anyway, but that I would be well prepared this time. I listened to a few of the opening jokes at the conference, and found a short one that I liked. Then I changed it to fit the audience I knew would be attending the FBI conference. I also typed it, word for word, on a note card.

I then approached a particularly good speaker after he gave a presentation and asked him if he always could capture the audience's attention the way he had done that day. He laughed and assured me that he had worked very hard to make it look effortless. I was relieved.

Before I gave my own lecture, I spent the afternoon in front of a mirror. I was visiting some friends in Washington. Due to my fear that I was going to make a fool of myself the next day, I gave up the fun of sightseeing in favor of practicing my talk. I forced myself to watch the mirror as I presented the information and practiced looking as if it was the easiest thing in the world for me to do. At one point, I kept stumbling over some words. I made myself repeat them several times until they were seamless. I also did a few run-throughs to make sure that I did not go over the twenty-minute time limit.

When it came time for me to do my presentation, I was nervous but ready. Because I had practiced so much, I did not have to read anything other than the headings for the topics I was presenting. I was able to walk around the stage, making eye contact with different people in the audience, the way I had seen the good presenters do at the other conference. I even *sauntered* at times. It felt so good. When it was over, I knew from the audience reaction that I really had nailed it. I had been able to inject the excitement I felt at that time regarding my work, even though it often seemed to be such a dry subject. I'll never forget one of the attendees, who had heard me speak on a prior occasion. He came up to me after this lecture and said, "Well, Robin, you really have come a *long* way. You used to be *so* boring and that was so interesting!"

The room was full of people who were in a position to help spread the word about my new tests and their strong results in predicting law enforcement officer performance. My company gained more than thirty new accounts over the next two years from this audience alone. My practice, motivated by fear of public embarrassment, had paid off.

Since that time, I realized that it was neither the joke nor the mirror practice that made my performance so successful. It was my relaxation over being so prepared and my understanding that I would no longer allow for crutches like fully written notes to save me. It also was my newfound ability to communicate directly with the audience that allowed participants to become more involved as I spoke. I was more comfortable with the knowledge of my subject and the security in knowing that I clearly had identified the most important points I wanted to make. This allowed me the freedom to show more of my personality in the presentation. I could be more attentive to what was going on around me and not appear as a worried stick figure in a suit.

Now I prefer practicing in front of a video camera in my room so that I can see how I present myself without trying to monitor techniques while I do them in a mirror. Since practice does make perfect in most situations, it is not a good idea to wait until the actual performance to make adjustments. Though very painful to watch, at times, I highly recommend the video feedback method. By watching yourself carefully in practice, it is easier to create performances where the foundations are prepared, but the delivery is spontaneous.

In any case, it is certain that we all will experience fearful situations in the future. In order to reduce future panic and head towards effective solutions faster, it is helpful to know that fear can be a strong motivator and can be channeled into high energy. This knowledge takes some of the sting out of the reality that something will come along in the future that will seem terrible, but actually will give us the boost we need to become motivated and act more quickly to solve problems. Of course, the ideal is to be able to turn on the high energy and focused motivation whenever we want to work towards a new goal. Most of us could do without the fear part.

To implement the **"U"** for **"Use Fear to Motivate Action"**:

1. Find something you are afraid of doing that could help you at work if you *could* do it. Write down why you think you can't do it.

2. Make a plan to do something new that you have been afraid of doing before. Break down what you want to do and divide the steps over several different sessions.

3. Start doing what you are afraid of doing today!

V – VISUALIZE YOURSELF AS A WINNER

"It's not how you win the game, but how you prepare to win"

... Bobby Knight

The game of tennis has taught me the importance of seeing yourself as a "winner" before you become involved in any competitive activity. Watching my children, and other children, in their various sports also has opened my eyes to the different ways people approach competitive events in their lives. If you watch any organized children's sports competition, whether it be Little League, hockey, gymnastics, or soccer, it does not take long to see which children are being raised to see themselves as winners and which children have the parents who criticize their every move, helping them to develop life-long feelings of inadequacy.

For the last two summers, I have been playing tennis with a man who is a very good tennis player, has a careful strategic style, and rarely gives up more than two or three games to me in a set despite my flailing efforts against him. Since tennis is a sport where there can be only one winner, the psychology is similar to many situations in business and personal life.

The other day, I realized that I was approaching my games with this man, who is almost ten years older than I am, with an uncharacteristic "loser's mentality." I know that he is a better technical player, but I lose points regularly that are due to a lack of self-confidence rather than to a lack of skill. Somehow, whenever I get ahead, especially after a few great serves, I have some kind of negative thought that I really couldn't be *that* good" and then I lose the next two or three games.

As in any sport, tennis is a game that takes years of practice to master. Since I only started playing a few years ago, I think that I am allowing unspoken beliefs such as "I'm unprepared for the big time" or "Somehow, I'm an imposter here" stop me from making a full-out "winner's" effort. Also, I once asked a tennis coach whether the best-trained women players could ever regularly win against the best males in this sport. Since the answer to my question was "no," due to lack of female upper body strength, I may have let that information color the way I view myself when playing against men, regardless of their skills or relative physical strength.

After I realized what I was saying to myself, I decided to change my approach. When the next day's set was at 5-1 in my opponent's favor, and I was behind in the next game at 15-40, I visualized myself making a great serve before each point. I started playing much better, concentrated harder, and won the next game, coming up from behind in a way that I had never done before against the three men who are willing to play tennis with me.

Even though my attitude alone couldn't change the good returns or serves my opponent sent my way, I was on a course of improvement. The next day, I decided to *start* with the more positive attitude. My opponent was playing very well that morning, yet I won the first game without giving away a single point and was ahead in the second game at 40-15 before I caved in to the 'old ways' and lost a few games. At least I was able to recognize the pattern. I laughed at myself for not being able to continue my more assertive style throughout the entire set, but also was pleased, having proven to myself for a few minutes that I had it *in me* to play that well.

Despite the fact that I still have not been able to win more than four games in a set with this man, I am enjoying the games and can see my psychological progress. By the end of the summer, and at the latest, next summer, I will visualize winning a set against this man and DO IT!

Examples of holding back on performance efforts due to feelings of inadequacy or feeling like an imposter are very common in the business world. I have seen some extreme cases of this in people who have difficulty managing others in their jobs both in the law enforcement field and in large corporations.

A psychologist who was a consultant for a large banking institution contacted my company to see if there was a good way to evaluate a high-level manager who wasn't performing well anymore. This man was in charge of two thousand employees and his bosses didn't understand what was happening with him. Apparently, he had been good at this same job for fifteen years and then, suddenly, was unable to handle his responsibilities. There was no question about drugs, alcohol, or family problems, and the psychologist already had used other tests to evaluate the presence of psychopathology or serious emotional adjustment difficulties. I suggested that the psychologist use one of my tests focusing on work ethic, social skills, learning ability, and social sensitivity.

The results were surprising and his test profile is one that stands out in my mind even though it has been years since this evaluation was completed. This manager showed very high academic ability. He was smart and able to learn quickly. He also had exceptional social skills. His test showed that he was personable, extroverted, and socially sensitive to the feelings of others. He even had a strong work ethic, leadership skills, and a well-developed sense of responsibility. From these tested characteristics, he appeared to possess the exceptional managerial potential that he actually had demonstrated on the job for so many years.

On this same profile, however, was one score that was unusually low and helped the psychologist to immediately focus in on the problem area. This man's self-worth or self-confidence score was nearly two standard deviations *below* the norm for entry-level job candidates. When he was questioned further, he admitted to the psychologist that, for years, he had "felt like an imposter." Even though others thought he was doing a good job, he believed that he had "no business" in such an important position. After many years, he had finally come to the decision that he didn't belong there and, with no faith in his own abilities, began to fail. This was the first time I had seen a case where a manager appeared to have every qualification except confidence.

Since then, I have watched for these profiles and investigated those I found in this category. I interviewed managers with similar test results and found that it didn't matter how talented they were at work. If, deep down, they didn't think they "belonged," then problems handling their jobs or getting along with others would surface. Managers with low self-confidence eventually would begin to display some kind of self-destructive behavior. I also noted that a higher percentage of females compared to males tend to show these low scores. At a human resources convention, I spoke with women in high-level positions who were amazed that my test could tell so much about them and their "secret" problem. If there is any truth to the saying that "a woman must work twice as hard to be seen as half as good," it is doubly hard when feelings of self-worth are at a premium.

In the law enforcement field, I also have seen this pattern, but with more serious consequences. Here, police officers with below average scores in self-confidence frequently become a liability for their departments. Officers often are evaluated for "fitness-for-duty" after an inappropriate shooting or incident when the officer's poor judgment has led to a negative result. Time and time again, the officer in question has endorsed test items to the effect that he or she tends to feel inferior in a group and does not have generally good feelings about him or herself.

In one case, a woman with extremely low scores in the areas of assertiveness and self-confidence on my tests was predicted to fail on the job as a public safety officer in the department I was consulting with at the time. Eventually, she was hired as a police officer by a different local agency that did not use this particular kind of psychological testing. Two years into the job, it came to our attention that she stood by as a group of male officers beat a civilian to death after he had committed a petty crime. While we could not predict exactly *how* her extremely low scores would manifest themselves, it was not surprising that she responded in this way when this unfortunate event occurred. The department that had rejected her at our suggestion marveled at how we had pinpointed the likelihood that she would "lack the appropriate assertiveness and confidence to be effective in the job of a police officer."

In a university-sponsored research study conducted several years ago, one of my tests developed specifically for adolescents was used with troubled high school students. Results showed that even a brief intervention program, geared to pointing out the teenager's good qualities and providing assertiveness training, helped to improve their test scores in the self-worth area.

Since it is a manager's job to assist employees in maximizing their potential, and, therefore, productivity, maintaining an atmosphere of support and positive reinforcement is as crucial in the workplace as it is in family life. Helping others to develop a winner's mentality, or the belief that "I can do what's expected of me and I can do it well," is a goal that can be reached as long as it is kept in mind.

Simple compliments based on *parts* of a job well done will encourage employees, as well as family members, to view their participation as useful and rewarding. They also will encourage further efforts to do the *whole* job well in the future. For example, my friend with her quilting business recently hired an assistant. The assistant knew how to sew, but not how to make quilts. When the assistant's first quilting efforts contained several mistakes, my friend complimented her assistant's knowledge of sewing in general and made statements about how, with these sewing abilities, the mistakes would be corrected in time.

Constant expression of the winner's attitude in your encouraging words to others *and* to yourself can keep feelings of inferiority at bay and enhance enjoyment of the work process for everyone involved.

To implement the "V" for "Visualize Yourself as a Winner":

1. Think of an area where you feel you need improvement. Visualize doing a task in that area better than you have ever done it before. Imagine yourself going through the details of that task and performing it in the way you have seen others do it well. Try to visualize yourself as the person you know who does it the way you would like to do it someday. Then imagine the good feeling of accomplishment that comes after making a successful effort. Promise yourself to remember that feeling the next time you actually are doing that task.

2. Make positive comments to three people in the next three days when you see them making an effort to improve on a skill. Be specific in your compliment and, as a practice exercise, don't make any suggestions for improvement at the same time unless the other person specifically asks for your assistance.

3. Make an effort to practice something you have difficulty doing today. Find three things you have done right in that effort, despite any mistakes, and compliment yourself out loud, specifically mentioning the parts you got right.

4. Remember that the Little League coach who calls out: "Good Effort!" when a child strikes out is a winner at a bigger game than the game being played that day. Make a resolution to give yourself this compliment every day.

W - WORDS CANNOT HARM YOU

"Find a Supportive Inner Circle without *Myrtles*"

Along the way to personal success, not everyone will be on your side. When insecure people become jealous, it is often because they do not know how to help themselves to reach their own goals. They may respond to your efforts to do something that helps you to reach your goals with derisive or purposefully hurtful remarks. Regardless of the reasons for their negative comments, the best defense is to deal with them in a positive way.

First, it is important to determine if a critical comment has any validity. Even when someone who is a little jealous of your success makes negative remarks, they may be useful to you. By taking a step back and asking yourself if you can learn anything from the comment, you may be able to find areas for self-improvement. One of the most successful leaders in industry today is well known for his tendency to question those around him relentlessly, soliciting their ideas, and even badgering them for advice.

Knowing whose words you usually can trust to be well-intentioned helps when you want to consult with an inner circle for information or feedback on how you are doing. This means that you must be vigilant in acknowledging backhanded compliments or self-serving comments that are made with the sometimes-unconscious intention of slowing you down. At times, the friends you develop at one point in your life are not able to remain friends as you develop further. They may be invested in their own lack of movement and will be negative and critical of any actions on your part to change.

Because there are usually some areas where everyone becomes a little defensive, you will maximize your chances for success by consulting with different people for different things. The best plan is to cultivate an inner circle of colleagues you can call on for advice. The people in this group do not necessarily have to be close friends. In fact, long-term friends or family members may not be the ones to give you the best advice when you are changing direction or making important life-altering decisions. This is not because they do not care about you, but rather that they may have a fixed view of who you are in relation to past situations that have no bearing on the present or future. It also is a good idea to watch for close associates whose special "buttons" you push by virtue of your specific activities.

For example, I have one colleague who I trust implicitly for advice and feedback in most areas. However, this colleague had a particularly difficult childhood that included both physical and emotional abuse. When looking back on her childhood, she rarely thinks of anything good. When I wrote and published my first songs, they were for children. These were happy, peppy songs that elicited a very negative response from this colleague. In fact, she didn't want to hear anything about my new venture and decided early on that I had no business trying to become involved with music.

Her strong negative reaction really was a reaction to her own childhood and to a feeling that, since her childhood was so difficult, she did not want to hear my happy children's songs. If I had listened to her advice, which was, "I don't think you should do this music," I would have missed one of the most gratifying parts of my life. Furthermore, when I began to write adult songs for myself to sing, this same colleague listened more carefully and decided that I wasn't lacking entirely in talent or good musical ideas after all.

Another colleague also had a strong negative reaction to the idea that I had started to write and record original music. When she made some derogatory comments, it was clear that there was more on her mind than that I wasn't attentive enough to my business or that I was a lousy singer or musician. In fact, this woman had wanted to be a concert violinist at one time. Her apparent dismay at my activities may have been due to disappointment at her own inaction regarding her musical interests. By watching the level of someone else's response, it is possible to recognize when there is more emotion attached to negative comments than your activities alone would be likely to generate. By recognizing a strong reaction in others as less related to you than to them, you can avoid feeling hurt by their negative comments.

On the other hand, it is important to be open to all criticism as a way to improve on your own performance. One of my friends recently finished writing her first novel. She sent it to some of her friends and asked them for comments. She asked for honest opinions and a critique of specific flaws in her work. Her open attitude led to her receiving constructive criticism that she could use to improve her book before sending it out to publishers. As she said, "I'm going to hear the negatives from the editors at book publishing companies eventually, anyway. I might as well be open to any comments, positive or negative, so that I can fix the mistakes now before I send my book out for professional review."

Recently, I performed a set of original songs with a full band in a Manhattan club. While I was thrilled to hear compliments from friends and family, I also welcomed the critical comments from other musicians. When more than one musician in the audience later suggested that I had sung the first few songs in keys that were too low for my voice, I devoted the summer to fixing this problem. A reluctance to raise the keys, for fear that I would not be able to hit the higher notes consistently, had been my reason for picking lower keys for these songs.

I then practiced these songs in increasingly higher keys, taping the results and listening back to how my vocals sounded. Forcing myself to listen to and do something about the suggestions that were both consistent and specific, including the one from the soundman who thought that I should get myself a better microphone, only made my next live performances better. Now I sing those particular songs with much more confidence, knowing that I have practiced enough to be able to hit those high notes *most* of the time. To match the attitude of the best Olympic performers, I now am working on changing that view of my high note abilities to *all* of the time.

The main point here is that one of the best ways to learn to do something better is to seek out and listen to expert advice. Being able to distinguish between advice that is meant to help you and comments that are subconsciously intended to hurt your progress is essential. A specific criticism tends to have more credibility that one that is more global (e.g. "Your drum tracks are terrible.") If you wish to learn what is wrong with something you have done, it is important to ask specifically for the advice you need.

Sometimes well-meaning and professional people do not give specific advice for fear of hurting someone's feelings or giving away "trade secrets." It is your job to ask enough questions about your performance in important skill areas so that you can elicit specific suggestions that will give direction to your next practice session. Practicing anything without constant guidelines for improvement will result only in the practicing of bad habits.

Finally, in your quest for discovering ways you can improve on the things you do, it is very important to identify the "Myrtles." A person nearly everyone has the misfortune of meeting at some time in his or her life, Myrtle can do a lot of damage if she gets her way. In my older daughter's case, Myrtle was a girl who transferred into her school during the eighth grade. Myrtle became friendly with my daughter and her best friend and they became an inseparable trio. Soon after their friendship began, however, Myrtle started to let slip several subtle "put-downs" aimed at my daughter. In an effort to be open and accommodating, my daughter accepted these comments without concern (such as "Oooo, You really *like* doing gymnastics? I always thought it was kind of silly" or "Your parents still make you practice piano? That's so dumb!")

As time went on, Myrtle convinced my daughter's best friend to stop hanging out with my daughter and to spend more time with her instead. As Myrtle convinced her friend to reject my daughter's friendship, my daughter was devastated. Taunting and negative comments became daily fare on the sidewalk after school. By the time my daughter's friend finally realized that Myrtle was the problem and was causing her to lose her best friend, it was too late. My daughter had found other kinder friends and, though she eventually resumed communicating with her first friend, their relationship never was the same. Two years later, after Myrtle had transferred schools again, my daughter heard a student there talking about how Myrtle had broken up friendships at her new school in the same way. That student had no idea that my daughter had been one of Myrtle's previous victims.

While it was very difficult at the time, the Myrtle incident taught my daughter a great deal. When she went on to high school, she immediately recognized anyone who made what we now call "a Myrtle," a comment or criticism that has no other intention than to hurt someone else. She steered clear of classmates who made such comments about others, occasionally telling me about them when she came home from school. Now a senior in high school, she has a circle of seven friends who are supportive and close with each other. It took her several years to build this network, but it is the kind that is likely to last past high school. The supportive comments I hear in their conversations assure me that wherever my daughter ends up in her life, she will know how to develop an inner circle of good friends to sustain her.

By becoming more aware of your "Myrtles" and "Myrtle Followers," you can anticipate their negative comments before being hurt by them. With increased vigilance, it becomes easier to identify those who habitually make subtle and not-so-subtle attempts to undermine or sabotage others. Once you can recognize "Myrtle's" insecurities for what they are, disapproving words cannot harm you. While avoiding these people is the best policy, there are times when you will have to find another solution. Learning to let criticism that does not offer specific ways for you to improve roll off of your back is an important coping skill. Separating constructive criticism from destructive criticism and choosing friends for your inner circle accordingly is another way to develop lasting harmony in your life.

To implement the **"W"** for **"Words Cannot Harm You"**:

1. Think about the most recent criticism you have received. Evaluate how you reacted to the comment. What did you learn about yourself? Did you learn something about the person who made the criticism?

2. Was there something specific that you did to correct your own behavior or performance? Is there something more that you would like to do in order to avoid similar criticism in the future?

3. List the people you consider to be in your "inner circle" at work. List the people in your "inner circle" in your personal life. Are any of them "Myrtles" or "Myrtle Followers?"

4. If you have a "Myrtle" in your life right now, make a resolution to avoid taking his or her negative remarks to heart without verification from others.

5. Make a plan to gather information from several sources before beginning self-improvement activities. Use a consensus of opinion to guide you in making major changes.

6. Think of a person who you would like to include in your inner circle. Make an effort to become closer with that person by inviting him or her to meet with you or socialize with you more frequently.

X – XPLORE NEW WAYS TO TAKE RESPONSIBILITY

"Be Part of the Solution, Not Part of the Problem"

Responsibility. This word that stands on its own seems to have lost its way in our society. The concept is an often cited, yet frequently overlooked, ideal that competes with the growing number of television confessionals and quick divorces. Along with the notion of responsibility comes its ally, respect. When we don't take responsibility for our actions, regardless of the "reasons" we may have found to justify them, we lose our self-respect. Without the knowledge that, deep down, after all is said and done, we have taken responsibility and done the "right thing," all eventually is lost. Money, power, real estate, sex, even the promise of everlasting youth cannot buy or build long-term happiness.

Yet, why is it so hard for people to incorporate this concept into their daily lives? Perhaps it is due to a fast-paced media that provides glimpses of desired paradise and then people's real lives fail to deliver. The disappointment that we cannot have everything we want exactly when we want it may contribute to some individuals taking what is wanted at any cost.

The recent movie, *"Duets,"* tries to deal with this issue as it explores the story of a father who did not take responsibility for his daughter and a husband who leaves his family in full-blown mid-life crisis "to get a cigarette." The husband's journey ends when he realizes that he should return to his understanding and loving wife. This happens after an innocent man has been killed and another man has given up his life, dying on screen as he tells the husband to "go home." This is a lot of drama and bloodshed that might have been avoided if the husband had made a genuine effort to talk with his wife in the first place.

In graduate school, I learned about several different techniques that have been successful in teaching children how to read. As a student seeking *the* correct solution to every problem, I soon became aware of the fact that there often are different options that can be used to get to the same place. The difference is in how much effort must be expended and how much trouble for you and others will be caused by each option in order to reach the end result. Taking responsibility tends to reduce the long-term fallout, though it can be painful and difficult at times.

A fascinating exercise is to listen carefully to other people as they talk about their problems. It is remarkable how often people blame others for situations they could avoid if they merely changed direction or entertained new options in their lives. Blaming others, while denying any responsibility for a situation, is one way to avoid facing the disappointment of personal failures or shortcomings. If someone else is to blame, then it may seem justifiable to spend time and energy trying to change that other person or at least complaining about their behavior. Of course, it is much easier to tell someone *else* to change, or to complain to a third party, than to change yourself. Putting the responsibility for life in other people's hands is not unusual, but it is costly.

As a psychologist, I frequently am asked to give my opinions about friends and relatives who are having problems. When I was getting my last haircut, my hairdresser asked me what I knew about fortunetellers. Her sister had been living a difficult life in Italy and had come to visit her in the U.S. Another of this hairdresser's customers is a fortuneteller and this woman had offered to read tarot cards for her sister. After trying out a few statements that would be correct for just about anyone, such as "you've had a hard life recently, a loss, perhaps," this fortuneteller had gotten the sister "hooked" on her predictions. The sister was calling my hairdresser from Italy, asking her to ask her fortuneteller client about every decision the sister was contemplating in her life. My hairdresser was concerned about her sister's new dependency and it started a conversation about how easy it is to think that someone else can or should be running your life.

Giving over responsibility is a habit that easily can be acquired by people after having difficult experiences that are not their "fault." For example, nearly everyone in jail today can recite a number of terrible things that happened to him or her that resulted in having to do jail time. However, not everyone from a tough background ends up in jail.

I know of one man who never has forgiven his mother for keeping him from playing football. Now in his forties, he doesn't allow his children to visit with their extended family because of his resentment. Actually, his anger is related to the fact that his father left his wife and six children to be with another woman. As decades passed and the father's actions became old news, this eldest son broke off with his relatives because, by not validating his concerns, they were taking away his excuse for not doing what he wanted to do in his life. When his siblings eventually carried on with their lives, without using their father's behavior as a crutch, this man could not stop talking about how he always had wanted to play football.

In relationships, refusal to take responsibility for one's actions often leads to a pattern of failures. One woman, who convinced her boss to leave his family to be with her, was distraught when this man finally left her, too. She wrote a letter to the man's daughter, claiming that it was the daughter's dislike of her that had created the friction leading to her separation from this man. Her letter did not acknowledge that her illicit relationship with this teenager's father had been the cause of the daughter's anger in the first place.

When there is a need to blame others in order to avoid responsibility, the convoluted thinking patterns that result can be quite amazing. I recently watched a woman's sunglasses fall off her head into the water as the motorboat she was riding in left the dock. This woman screamed at her husband that he had left the dock too quickly and that was why she hadn't been prepared for the wind that blew her hat that knocked the glasses off. It was entirely *his* fault even though she later admitted that she had not had time that month to put the clips on that she usually used to hold her glasses onto her head!

Taking responsibility means to evaluate carefully what role, if any, you have played in creating a problem. The next step is to work to solve that problem in a direct and honest manner. Another aspect of responsibility is to know when you must give up control and allow others to solve their problems without your intervention.

A woman recently asked for my opinion about her adult son, who had behaved violently towards his girlfriend. She had become involved in their arguments in the past, trying to help the girlfriend cope with her son, who still was living at home. She felt responsible for the fighting and wanted to do something. We talked about how it was her son, and not her, who needed to take responsibility for his actions. It would be more productive for her to set limits about the activities that would be allowed inside her home, such as physical fighting. Asking her son to live elsewhere and offering to provide professional counseling were options she could consider, but becoming involved in the details of her son's difficulties most likely would lead to further arguments and frustration.

As I was writing this chapter, my youngest daughter came into the room and asked if I would call her ballet teacher to explain why she couldn't attend class that day. Perhaps because of the subject I was writing about at the time, I explained that it was time she took responsibility for her schedule and made the cancellation herself. She expressed concern that her teacher would not believe that she had a valid reason to miss her dance class. I encouraged her to pick up the phone and she was successful in telling her teacher about her need to study that night for her first biology test. When she hung up the phone, she remarked, "That wasn't so hard after all!"

To implement the "X" for **"Xplore New Ways to Take Responsibility"**:

1. Think of the worst problem that you have at this time. List all of the possible ways that you may have contributed to making the situation more difficult.

2. Write a list of the possible outcomes if you do nothing about this problem.

3. List the various outcomes or solutions that can result from your future actions related to this problem.

4. Write a full description of the action you plan to take first. Then list additional actions you will take if the first action does not result in an acceptable solution.

5. Take responsibility for this problem today by acting on the plan you described above. Set a time limit so that you will know when to evaluate the results of your action. Then continue to take responsibility by adding the additional actions as necessary along with set times when you will evaluate the outcome.

6. Write a list of five problems that have been of concern to you that are *not* your responsibility. Make a resolution to focus on your problems and to leave these problems for others to solve.

Y – YOU ARE WHERE YOU ARE

**"...Grant us the serenity to accept what cannot be changed,
The courage to change what can be changed;
And wisdom to know one from the other"**

...Reinhold Niebuhr

In a college acting class, one of my classmates said something that was viewed as naïve and arrogant by the instructor who was teaching the course. This classmate apparently had implied by her comment that her future was wide open and that there were endless possibilities. Perhaps the acting teacher had felt threatened by this since he had recently moved to a university located in a fairly isolated area after failing to make an acting career for himself in New York City. He stopped the class and berated her for being so sure of herself and having such an idealistic view about her future.

I remember clearly how it hit me that he was right when he said something like, "My dear, you, too, will find yourself somewhere specific twenty years from now. You'll be living in only one place, in only one town, in a house somewhere, probably using a fork to eat your food, doing ordinary things and living an ordinary life." I thought that he was being mean to the student, but his point was interesting: You have to be *somewhere* at every moment in your life and that somewhere may turn out to be pretty mundane and/or miraculous depending on how it is analyzed.

Over twenty years later, I was sitting in another classroom in a different college, this time accompanying my teenagers as they attended their weekend music classes. Thinking back, I might have been horrified if I had known that the place I would be in twenty years was simply another college classroom.

In any case, this class was music theory, which is a difficult subject to teach to a group of students since different students often know much more than others depending on which aspect of theory is being discussed. The teacher was trying to determine which students were having trouble in a particular area. One student, a highly talented trumpet player, was having a great deal of difficulty doing an exercise that others in the class could do easily. He appeared to be very embarrassed at this, and the teacher stopped the class to tell us her story.

She described how she had experienced tremendous stress in her own college music studies. She had studied with a teacher, similar to my old acting teacher, who apparently enjoyed scolding and making fun of students who didn't understand something. After enduring his negative remarks, she decided that when she became a teacher, it would be different. She carefully explained to the junior and senior high school students in her class that morning that "you are where you are" in life. Yes, you only can be in one place at a time and that place may not be exactly where you *want* to be. However, when you accept that it is O.K. to be wherever you are, especially on a learning curve that is different for each person in every subject, you then can move forward.

She carefully explained to this trumpet student that it was not a failing on his part that he didn't know how to do something, like sing a type of music scale. Her job as a teacher simply was to find out where he needed help and then to provide it. No one else in the class could play the trumpet and he needn't feel inferior about *anything*. All that was necessary was for him to make a good effort to learn.

Remembering this simple sentence has since helped me to progress in my favorite "hobby." As I listen to people who are better performers, singers, guitarists etc., all the things I would like to learn to do better, I repeat, "You are where you are" and that reduces the pressure to be perfect at something right away. Accepting the limitations of what you can be at any given moment is not the same as giving up on a glorious future of success in that area. This idea allows me to give myself the freedom to explore new areas without allowing myself to feel intimidated by others who may be able to do better than me in those areas.

With more free time and affluence in our society, there is increasing competition at the high end of many activities. I know of two high school girls, overwhelmed by the pressure to succeed, who made suicide attempts last year as a way to relieve the stress they felt at "having" to get top grades at all times. With family problems at the root of their insecurities, their self-imposed pressure to excel in school became too much for them to bear.

While working hard is necessary for success, keeping balance and moderation by programming time to do other things is essential. It is comforting to be able to relax with the concept that there always will be someone better and worse than you are at anything you try. Even the best performers are outdone eventually by their age or by the increased abilities of others who copy their success. Taking away the unrealistic pressure to be the best forever can allow for slower, but long-term, positive results. Running the race only against yourself, and giving yourself the option to be bad at times, does much to relieve the pressure.

Finally, just because you may find yourself in a predictable, or perhaps even boring, place today does not mean that you won't be in an exciting position tomorrow. By keeping yourself centered and focused on exactly where you are today, you are in the best possible position to complete the next step of your "to do" list. One situation taught me that remarkable increases in knowledge or experience can occur overnight, provided that you are open to the idea of making quick adjustments.

During the early years of building my business, I attended monthly meetings of security directors in a large city. Several companies were beginning to use some of my tests and I had convinced the manager of the local branch of a large national contract guard company to use our services.

At one of these Friday afternoon luncheons, I was standing with a group of corporate security directors. In front of this group, my new client asked, "Do you like football?" Trying to be "cool" with the men surrounding me, I answered, "Yes, sure," even though my previous experience with football had been a few marches down the field while playing the flute in my high school band. I never had watched the games and my entire understanding about how football was played was that touchdowns were very important.

My client then told me that his company had chartered a bus for the next day and that he would like it very much if I would join his staff in attending the Army-Navy game along with their major customers, all male security directors from large corporations. Now I had really done it. Here was a golden opportunity to develop relationships with important clients. However, I was going to be sitting with "the boys" all afternoon in twenty-degree weather. If I didn't have a clue about what was going on during the game, it was bound to be boring, freezing, and potentially embarrassing. As a "professional businesswoman," I had no desire to appear ignorant about something these men took so seriously.

Taking stock of "where I was" wasn't very difficult. I knew nothing. Figuring out what to do about it precipitated a flurry of activity for the next sixteen hours. Basically, I decided that to move from "where I was" to "where I wanted to be" required learning the details of how football was played overnight. First, I went home and spent one hour with a female friend trying to figure out what I could wear to this event that would be casual, yet professional, and warm enough to withstand hours outside in the unusually cold weather. I decided on a long wool skirt and sweater that would hide my flannel ski underwear underneath.

When my husband came home from work, he drew me a diagram of the football field and marked each position of the players as he explained their primary functions on the team. Then he went out to our local bookstore and bought me a copy of John Madden's book, *One Knee Equals Two Feet (And Everything Else You Need to Know About Football)*. Now I had my work cut out for me. I spent the evening reading this book and memorizing the diagram. Since I had to meet the company bus by eight the next morning, I only put the book down to sleep a few hours and to take a shower. The effort paid off.

The next day, I was ready to "talk football" or at least to listen with some idea of the language that was being spoken. I decided that my best strategy was to be quiet unless asked a question. I also decided that I would root for Navy, only because I liked to sail. When I got on the bus, there were a few women joining us. One worked for the company and was an avid football fan while the others were disinterested wives of the guests.

My client introduced me to his guests and, as they talked, I realized that a company employee who had attended West Point had obtained the tickets for this game. Already, I had chosen to root for the wrong team! I kept this to myself as we headed for the stands wearing special Army hats in eighteen-degree weather. Normally, if I am outside in this climate, I am quickly maneuvering down an alpine ski hill on the way to a warm lodge. I really had trouble appreciating the concept of standing still in the cold so that I could watch other people run around. Nonetheless, for the next few hours, I followed the game with great interest. It was fun to recognize some of the plays and football jargon I had crammed into my brain the previous night. Such concentration also helped to ward off the cold.

By half time, the two or three women in our party decided to call it quits and head for the warm bus. They made a point of inviting me to come along as they left their husbands behind. I graciously declined their offer saying, "Oh, no. I'll stay here. I really want to watch the game!" As they left, the bank director on my left turned to me and, in football talk, said, "Can you *believe* that?! My wife didn't even know what "=234$%^$%^" was!" I had to type nonsense here because I didn't know what he was talking about then and I certainly can't remember what he said now. However, I smiled at him in knowing agreement that anyone who didn't know what *that* was couldn't be taken very seriously!

As I was chatting with another bank director, sitting on my right, I let it slip that I secretly had been rooting for Navy. He was thrilled and said that he was a Navy man, too. I wasn't doing too badly so far. After what seemed like forever, the freezing game finally was over and it was time to return to the bus. The host of the party had returned to the bus earlier in order to prepare some food for the guests, and I figured he would ask me how I had enjoyed the game. On the walk back through the crowd, I listened carefully to what was going on around me. When I heard some men discussing the details of the game, I slowed my pace and walked in front of them so that I could hear what they were saying. After learning what Army had done wrong, I headed for our bus. Almost on cue, my client immediately asked me what I thought of the game and I answered, "Well, it was good, but I think Army ran too much with the ball." He nodded in wholehearted approval and I nearly laughed out loud thinking "*what a difference a day makes.*"

Since that day, I watch TV football with an entirely different attitude. Whenever I see steam rising from a player's breath, I am grateful that I am not sitting there in the stands. I also remember how spending that night with a book on the rudiments of football helped me to make friends in business.

To implement the **"Y"** for **"You Are Where You Are"**:

1. Note an activity or area of study where you probably would fall in the middle of a group of friends if you were compared on your relative abilities in this area.

Note an activity where you would fall at the top and another where you would fall at the bottom when compared with this same group of friends.

2. Remember that no matter how hard you try, you never are required to know or to learn everything.

3. Make a resolution to accept "where you are" and to move forward from that position with a positive attitude.

4. Pick a subject or activity about which you know very little and ask a friend to teach you the basics. Buy a book about the same subject and discuss it with your friend. Then put yourself in a place where you can use this new knowledge, such as a club meeting or sports event.

Z – ZEST FOR LIFE GIVES US POWER

"This little guiding light of mine, I'm going to let it shine.
This little guiding light of mine, I'm going to let it shine...
Hide it under a bushel, no! I'm going to let it shine...
Let it shine all the time. Let it shine."

... Traditional camp song

Seeking your passion in life is something that can be elusive but, perhaps, one of the most worthwhile efforts you can make. It is a lucky person who is able to spend most of the day doing what he or she loves and this is not always by accident. Knowing about and arranging for yourself to do what makes you happy may be a process just like anything else. Sacrifices may be required as you spend the necessary time following dead ends or working on the wrong skills or wrong job on your journey to finding your own "light under a bushel."

Recently I was attending a large county fair and wandered into the farm museum. As I was looking around, a man approached me and asked if I would like to know about the huge antique wheel that was part of some equipment used to butcher cattle in the early 1900's. When I asked him a few questions, he was excited to tell me all about the lifestyle on his farm when he was a boy during the Depression. After working all day on the farm, he and his brothers would take ten to twelve cattle to be "dressed down" using this type of machinery. As the man, who said he was known as 'Doc,' spoke, his expression told me that he had good memories of his experiences on the farm.

Doc asked me how old I thought he was. At eighty-six, he looked to be in his early seventies. He still was working, though he said that his main job now is "only to fill trenches with silage brought in by the big trucks and cover them over with large tarps." Doc once had won an award from the state soil conservation department for laying over nine miles of drainage pipe in an area that needed that work. Married for fifty-seven years until his wife died, this farmer said that he had gone through the eighth grade in school. He told me how he loved farm work and looked forward to working everyday. He had started his career by working for another farmer before buying his own farm with fourteen cows. This coming winter, he was proud to say that he and his son were hoping to milk two hundred cows.

Doc was fortunate in that he had good memories to share and goals to reach. He created both his memories and goals with his zest for life and keen interest in what he was doing. His conversation was fascinating to me, largely due to his enthusiasm and obvious passion for farming. When he told me that five of his six siblings were alive and well, with the youngest now only eighty, I asked him what was the secret to his long and healthy life. His response was not surprising, but worth repeating.

First, he talked about relationships. He said, "Stay with the one you're with. This fence jumping is no good. If you want to make it, it's more give than take and it's important not to ever go to bed angry." Second, he spoke about lifestyle. "Eat good food. If you can grow it yourself, that's the best way. I'm looking for a woman now who is even-tempered so we can get along, doesn't smoke, and doesn't drink much. I haven't found her yet, though." Next, he talked about work. "If there's work to do, do it. It's no good to sit around. You have something to do, so do it," he commented. Doc had learned early to be wise about the need for balance and compromise. He had worked hard, had a loving family, had been recognized for his accomplishments, and was proud of himself. All of this with a passion for living that had not died, despite the fact that he clearly missed his wife.

If you can find your passion, you can amuse yourself for the rest of your life. I have met several other people who have managed to work at what they love and play whenever they work. One afternoon, I had the opportunity to sail with a man in his seventies who walked down to the water with some boards tucked under his arms. Some young boys and I watched as he unfolded the boards and they became a hinged dinghy to be used to get to his sailboat that was moored in the bay. The boys were amazed and one asked, "Hey, Mister, where did you buy that boat?" He chuckled as he answered, "I didn't buy it. I made it!"

This man built sailboats from scratch and was known around the City Island area as a master boat builder. When he retired, he sailed across the ocean without a motor on a twenty-two-foot sailboat that he had built himself. He made a movie about his voyage that included a few raging storms and being stranded in the ocean for two weeks without food. When a large ship offered to take him aboard, he declined, saying, "Thank you very much for your help, but you aren't headed in my same direction!" He was proud that he had been featured in *Ripley's Believe It or Not* for sailing the smallest sailboat across the ocean without a motor. In order to prove that this wasn't a fluke, he sailed another boat across the Atlantic a few years later.

Another resourceful person who was able to make his dreams come true later in life was a shop and agricultural teacher in a school system for thirty-two years. When he retired, he wanted to buy some rental property for extra income. In the process of doing this, he came upon an old gristmill that had been abandoned at the turn of the century. It became his dream and passion to restore this mill to working condition and to provide a museum for the public to enjoy. After five years, he was able to restart the mill with the help of a dozen of his neighbors and friends. Now in his eighties, he still gives tours of this mill, making the big wheel turn even as his knees are giving out. He recently has published a book about the mill's restoration and his enthusiasm is catching as he speaks about times when getting cornmeal and winter feed for farm animals was a full day's work. His love of teaching and of what he is doing is apparent as he comments how he was "the luckiest man in the world" because he was able to find the original wheel patterns in the old ruins of the mill. A few years ago, his community honored this man's contribution by naming the local elementary school after him.

Some people are able to find what they love at a very young age. Then they spend their lives devoted to that passion, at least until another one develops. My older daughter, now seventeen, is one of those people. It has been fascinating to watch her enjoyment of an activity that she now has been involved with for over ten years.

At the age of six, my daughter first went inside a local gymnastics school to pick up her brother and his friend. A neighbor had suggested that I sign my eight-year-old son up for a few months of gymnastics along with her son. Neither of them wanted to continue after those months were over. However, as soon as my daughter saw the other children tumbling and jumping around, she was hooked. She begged me to let her take lessons too, and I refused for a whole year. I knew there would be many activities for her to become involved with and I didn't want to start her on something like this until she was at least seven or eight. Our family had no connection with gymnastics and I had my own plans for her to study other subjects instead. However, every time she heard about or thought about gymnastics, she would beg to be allowed to go to the gym. Finally, I told her she could go when she turned seven.

On the first day, while waiting to be evaluated by a coach, she ran onto the mat and started throwing herself into a cartwheel without hands, an "aerial," just as she saw some other girls doing at the time. When the coach came back to talk with me, she asked where my daughter had trained previously. When I answered that she hadn't trained anywhere, the coach asked me the same question two more times before giving me a weird look and a shrug. I knew she didn't believe me because of my daughter's enthusiasm, natural coordination, and willingness to try anything. Years later, after my daughter became a high level gymnast, we laughed about that day.

To make a long story short, this child spent the next ten years practicing gymnastics. Unlike most other girls in her gym, she was self-motivated and determined to do her sport regardless of the obstacles in her way. We never had to look for an effective way to punish this daughter since she would respond immediately to the threat of "O.K. If this is how you are going to behave, then no gymnastics today!"

On several occasions, we asked her to consider quitting. At the age of eleven, she fractured her back during a competition and had to spend nine months wearing a plastic back brace. She refused to quit, went back to the gym, and became the New York State Level 8 All-Around Champion three years later. Each time we asked her to consider retiring from the sport, she explained that she had certain goals that she wanted to meet first. She now has met most of them. She attended two Level 9 Regional Junior Olympics, and brought medals home from both competitions. She currently competes as a Level 10 gymnast, her stated goal years ago. Although my husband is in the field of physical rehabilitation, and never has been a fan of artistic gymnastics because of its injuries, even he could not refuse this daughter's request to continue with a sport she obviously loved so much. We were pleased, however, when we were successful in convincing our younger daughter to pursue the less dangerous sport of rhythmic gymnastics.

Since most children jump from one activity to the next, we underestimated the amount of commitment and passion that *is* possible in a young child. My daughter now is applying to college and does not wish to consider any schools that do not have a competing girl's gymnastics team. Knowing that she will have only four years left to practice this sport as a bona fide competitor, she already has signed up to take the course required to become a gymnastics competition judge. She talks about wanting to be the kind of judge who smiles at the competitors, giving them encouragement and a good feeling about their efforts, just as some judges have given her. This is her plan for continuing in her sport as an adult even if she eventually works at a different professional career.

My daughter's passion has been difficult to handle at times. She rarely has been at home during the normal dinner hour. However, what she has shown us about a love for a process ("I just love to tumble and work-out") and a commitment to excellence ("I want to be a Level 10") has made us proud to have a daughter who can teach us so much about how to live a dream.

Of course, most people do not find their major interests so easily. Being open to new experiences and trying many different things throughout the years eventually can bring the satisfaction and joy in life that we each seek.

For some people, different stages in life bring different passions and activities. My own greatest passion so far has been music and songwriting. However, unlike my daughter, it took until I already was in my forties for me to discover this and to have the ability to do something about it. I have found that it is never too late to develop a new interest *if* you can accept the idea that you may have to start from scratch. You also may have to put other things aside temporarily when you begin a new venture.

While I can look back now and wish that I had known about my connection with songwriting earlier, I probably would not have had the freedom to explore it fully in past years. When I was younger, professional recording of original music was reserved only for signed artists on major record labels. It is only in recent years that there has been a tremendous boost to independent musicians and songwriters by the modern technology of the Internet and affordable recording equipment. Also, I enjoyed building my testing business for many years, a passion that once required sixty to eighty hour weeks. With the competing desire to enjoy family life as well, I know that I never could have done it all at the same time.

It is important to realize that "having it all" does not necessarily mean "having it all" at once. If you view your life as an unfolding tale, filled with side plots and turns, then your gathering of "it all" comes gradually as you mature and are able to decide what it is that you really want. At this time, I now have the opportunity to indulge in my songwriting passion using all of the knowledge I finally have gained from experiences with prior interests and activities.

For example, I started my young adult life being interested in theatre. There was a time when I could not understand how it was that not everyone wanted to be an actor on stage. While I was attending graduate school, I performed in over a dozen "off-off" Broadway shows. These shows provided me with the relief from studying I desperately needed. Also, when I was in a show and could explore how the character I was playing thought and behaved, I was thrilled. This character analysis really was an exercise in psychology, a field that became my focus a few years later.

However, passions will be tempered by a person's ability to fulfill them. Since I really couldn't sing or dance well, and most Broadway shows were musicals at the time, there was limited paying work available to me in New York theatre. I did perform leading roles in some dinner theatre shows and realized that if I wanted to continue being paid to act, I would have to be willing to travel extensively. Since I also wanted to have children within a few years, I made the conscious decision to cut back on my involvement in theatre and concentrate more on the psychological work I was doing at the time. It is ironic that I ended up traveling more for my psychology career than I probably ever would have done if I had continued in acting. In fact, my younger daughter accompanied me on nine round-trip plane rides before she was nine months old! It is important to note that although I never starred on Broadway, my New York acting experience and training has made standing on stage to give a lecture or to perform my music a lot easier for me now.

Following your passion, when you have discovered what it *is*, can be one of the most satisfying adventures in life. However, even people who swear that their passion is "only a hobby" usually have some goals that they would like to reach in that area. It is important to keep in mind that you may have to work harder than ever before to reach your goals related to a passion. Passion-related goals usually are elevated compared to other goals, since people tend to set higher standards for themselves when they really care about something. Sometimes it is better to "kick back" for a little while and indulge in the activity you love with no other goal than pure relaxation and enjoyment.

As you find the joy in your passions and enjoy the effort you put into them, so will those around you. Even if other people do not understand exactly why you have chosen a particular activity, they, too, will become excited by your enthusiasm and support your efforts when they realize the joy it brings you to follow a dream.

While I've focused here on following passions as a way to bring joy to your life, zest for life really comes with the understanding and practice of the following idea: It is the *combination* of maintaining strong positive relationships with those we love *and* maintaining strong positive relationships with the things we do that brings the greatest satisfaction in life. As we each continue our quest to find that satisfaction and "have it all," I wish you a most joyous journey!

To implement the **"Z"** for **Zest for Life Brings Us Power**:

Set aside time today to follow your dreams!

About the Author...

Dr. Robin Inwald is the founder and director of Hilson Research, Inc., a psychological test publishing company that focuses on the development of specialized employment tests. The author of over fifty psychological tests, Dr. Inwald has written numerous published academic articles and book chapters. Her comments on various issues have appeared in media as diverse as the *New York Times*, *Wall Street Journal*, *Redbook*, *Men's Health*, *Cosmopolitan* magazines, and *CBS News*. She has written guidelines for practice in the police psychology field that have been adapted for use by professional psychological organizations. She also was a special consultant to the American Psychological Association and to a congressional committee in their efforts to understand and regulate psychological testing and laws such as the Americans with Disabilities Act and the Civil Rights Act of 1991. Since 1985, Dr. Inwald has been a Diplomate in Forensic Psychology, one of approximately 150 psychologists nationwide who is recognized by the American Psychological Association's American Board of Professional Psychology and the American Board of Forensic Psychology as having expertise in the area of psychology and the law. In 1995, she was invited to become a founding member of the American Board of Assessment Psychology. She frequently is consulted as an expert witness in police psychology and in cases involving testing issues. Dr. Inwald received a bachelor's degree in theatre arts and English from Cornell University, a Ph.D. from Columbia University, and Certificates in Illustration & Fine Art from Parsons School of Design. This year, the New York State Psychological Association presented her with the *2000 David C. McClelland Award* for "meritorious achievement in psychology."

For Additional Copies of

How to Have it All and Keep Your Sanity,

Call **800-926-2258** or visit the Hilson Web site at

HilsonResearch.com

Also available by the same author:

ABC's for Inner Strength & Well-Being

A book written for adults who are dealing with trauma, illness, or an emotional crisis. Readers are provided with an easy reminder of how to lead a balanced life and maintain inner strength.

Cap It Off With a Smile: A Guide for Making Friends

Children of all ages want to have friends but many are unsure of how to make them. This four-color illustrated children's book uses the acronym "CAPS" to help children make friends and maintain lasting relationships. Suitable for ages 3-12.

Other CAPS Materials Include:
CAPS Activity Workbook
CAPS Songs for Friendship Tapes
CAPS T-shirts, hats & buttons
Spanish versions of book and workbook

Mini-Hilson Personnel Profile/Success Quotient

A ten-minute inventory appropriate for ages 15 and up. Designed for use in career assessment to aid in the identification of work-related strengths and weaknesses. Self-administered and self-scored.

To hear Robin Inwald's music, visit her web site at:

RobinInwald.com

or call **800-926-2258**

CDs Currently Available Include:

Electricity (adult pop)

If I Feel Like It (adult pop single)

A River's Story (adult contemporary/pop)

"Where the river ends is where I'm going,
To recover from the love I've lost,
'Cause what seems to be the end
Is really just the river's bend,
And a new way is worth all its cost."

Robin Inwald
"Take My Hand" from *A River's Story*